CASE STUDIES IN CROWD MANAGEMENT

Chris Kemp
Iain Hill
Mick Upton
Mark Hamilton

ENTERTAINMENT TECHNOLOGY PRESS

Safety Series

CASE STUDIES IN CROWD MANAGEMENT

Chris Kemp, Iain Hill, Mick Upton, Mark Hamilton

Entertainment Technology Press

Case Studies in Crowd Management

© Chris Kemp, Iain Hill, Mick Upton, Mark Hamilton

First Edition Published July 2007 by
Entertainment Technology Press Ltd
The Studio, High Green, Great Shelford, Cambridge CB22 5EG
Internet: www.etnow.com

ISBN 978 1 904031 48 2

A title within the
Entertainment Technology Press Safety Series
Series editor: John Offord
in association with Buckinghamshire New University

CODE / CSCM01-0108

CONTENTS

4 A CROWD SAFETY MANAGEMENT PLAN FOR AN OUTDOOR ROCK CONCERT EVENT WITH AN ATTENDANCE OF 60,000 PERSONS

ACKNOWLEDGEMENTS

With thanks to the project's research assistants:

Holly Piggott
Danyka Barke
Natalie Gorohova
Sarah Bartholomew
Matt Kinsley
Claire McLeod
Rebecca Fowles
Carly Spinner
Lyndsey Patterson
Shirin Easson
Guy Valerino
Ray Browning
Luke Westbury
John-Paul Greenock
Lisa Glendenning
Jennie Gill
Matt Street
Warren Tucker
Aimee Murzell
Kathryn Braddick
Sam Clegg
Ade Goldsmith
Anna Koblizek
Dr Mandla Nyathi

INTRODUCTION

This book has been compiled from a series of research projects carried out by the staff of the Centre for Crowd Management and Security Studies and seminar work carried out in Berlin and Groningen with our partner Yourope.

It was clear from the outset that a credible academic research programme was only likely to be accepted by the industry if it could be understood by those at the forefront of event safety management. To produce academic work without a focus on the practical and vocational would not suffice. The introduction of the Licensing Act of 2003 pushed the industry and academia closer together and as such enabled the Centre to enhance its project possibilities.

The Centre was also well placed to support the training needs of the crowd management and health and safety industry. By the creation of a number of bespoke qualifications linked to governing body and other awards the centre found a niche which allowed research and training to flourish in a supportive environment. These developments lead to the creation in 2003 of a Foundation Degree in Crowd Management and then to subsequent Foundation degrees in Protective Security and Security Systems Management. As well as Foundation Degree programmes the centre has supported qualifications endorsed by the Security Industry Authority and has created programmes in Pit Training and Security Consultancy as well and engineering a partnership programme at masters level and undergraduate programmes combining policing and security.

The previous published report by the centre was an attempt to measure the various processes that make up the ingress and egress in a major outdoor concert event and to validate or refute these findings by means of a comparison between what was perceived as being two very distinct audiences: that of Eminem at the Milton Keynes Bowl and the Robbie Williams audience that attended his record-breaking shows at Knebworth House in the summer of 2003.

The particular attraction of the Knebworth site lies in its status as a complete green-field site. The project set out to develop its own particular research tool which consisted in adapting an Excel spreadsheet for use in converting flow measurements from a limited number of ingress gates, into an estimate of both the aggregate flow of the audience into the venue during the previous hour and also of the cumulative total figure of the audience that had entered the arena at any given point during the ingress procedure.

It was at this point, during the first trial run of the process, that the first major findings emerged. At around 18:30 hours, with less than 90 minutes before the headlining artist was due to go onstage, the cumulative reading was that there were only a little more than 110,000 people inside the arena out of a total capacity of 125,000. This implied that 15,000 people were still to arrive at the venue and that the process of standing down or converting the emergency exits into ingress gates would have to be delayed to accommodate those still making their way in. Yet all the other indicators suggested that there was something amiss with the spreadsheet, that the results being given were incorrect or distorted; experience suggested that it was very rare indeed for so many people to arrive so late for a concert where although the main artist was still to appear, there was a significant array of other major acts as support to the main event. Furthermore, the traffic reports coming in from the police to the Command and Control Centre were suggesting that all was normal. Finally, visual evidence taken from the vantage point of the control room showed that the arena was practically full, as would normally be expected at this time. However, the audience continued to arrive, indicating that the trickle that would normally be expected at this point of the ingress procedure, was in fact a steady flow.

What eventually emerged from enquiries into the concert flow calculations was the picture of the chaos that the concert audience had caused on the northbound carriageway of the A1M, swamping the normal congestion of the Friday afternoon rush-hour, and compounded by inappropriate signposting on the motorway that had combined to turn the whole approach to the area by road into one huge traffic jam. This still had not cleared by the time the concert was approaching its final half hour. The press became involved in the ensuing chaos and the organisers and those associated with the event learned the lesson of the impracticability of staging an event of this magnitude in close proximity to London with limited public transport links. What worked at the Reading Festival proved not to work at a site in rural Hertfordshire.

These facts served to validate the findings of the research team. The spreadsheet tool had not been inaccurate as was first presumed; on the contrary it had served its purpose in identifying and highlighting a significant deviation from the norm in terms of the amount of people in the arena at a given point in time; a point in time when the crowd management team would be making significant decisions to convert ingress gates into exits and standing down the personnel carrying out the ingress checks. The results of this comparative research project were published by Entertainment Technology Press in 2004 (*A Comparative Study of Crowd Behaviour at Two Major Music Events*).

This book focuses on a series of case studies, each unique but leading to a series of results and conclusions which provide issues for dialogue and further research. Chapter 1 focuses on a case study which looks at the deaths at Donnington Park during the Monsters of Rock event in 1988 written by the Head of Security at the Event. This case study is included as a comparison of events within the book and to highlight the changes that have taken place since this event.

This report was one of the original inspirations for the approach to the research projects instigated by BCUC published as a result of an investigation into an incident that ended in the deaths of two members of the audience at the Castle Donnington Monsters of Rock Festival in 1988. It identifies major issues at that time. In this report the author, Mick Upton, outlines the concept of a crowd surge within the context of a large outdoor festival and details the events that led to this tragic surge: the meteoric rise in popularity of one of the artists, Guns 'n' Roses, who had not justified headliner status when the festival had been booked but who had attracted a large portion of the audience to the show, all of whom wanted to push towards the front of stage as the band prepared to begin their set, the first time they had performed in the UK. This surge, combined with the poor conditions underfoot as a result of a previous downpour, had tragic consequences. The long-term importance of the report was seen, however in the impetus that the events at Castle Donnington gave to the creation of the *Event Safety Guide*, otherwise known as 'The Purple Guide' a document published by the Health and Safety Executive that has been the manual for the safe staging of concert events in the UK since its first publication.

Chapter 2 focuses on the Red Hot Chilli peppers gig at Hyde Park in London on June the 19th & 20th 2004. This case study focuses on the crowd build up at the event, flow capacities and observations and the findings from the questionnaires distributed at the Event.

In Chapter 3 we see a further publication based on the results of this line of research where the Cumulative Audience Spreadsheet, to give it a name, was being used to help the organisers of the VE Day Memorial concert in Trafalgar Square decide whether to open the gates to the non-ticket holding public that had gathered around the Square, but had been kept outside the arena. With 15 minutes to go before the event started, it was clear that of the 15,000 people that had applied for free tickets through personal applications, only just over half that number had entered arena. Armed with an estimate based on the spreadsheet taken form the 'clicker' counts provided by the security team in place on the ingress gates, combined with clear visual evidence of the crowd density within the arena, the organisers and the crowd management team, in consultation with the emergency liaison team, decided to remove the restriction on ticket holders up until a point where the arena was filled to its 15,000 licensed capacity.

As can be seen from this chapter, the full scope of the report commissioned is has a wider remit than that outlined above. It attempted to appraise the viability of holding free open-air concerts in Trafalgar Square from a viewpoint that focused on but was not limited to safety issues. Another facet of the research project is the detailed use of questionnaires in an attempt to monitor the mood of the audience at this event. The scope of the questionnaires is far beyond assessing whether the audience is enjoying the event; rather it seeks to establish the audiences' awareness of their personal safety and comfort and to put this in the context of the broader concert environment. The research aims to establish the degree to which the audience feels secure within the environment provided by the event organiser, and then to determine the premise on which that security (or lack of it) is founded.

This type of research, and the ability of the Centre's research team to extract representative (in statistical terms) samples of the audience, is a key contribution to the program as a whole. The ability to illustrate the audience's attitude in respect of specific issues including the way that the ingress procedure is managed and to gauge audience awareness of some of the environmental issues that are likely to affect attendees throughout the day (weather conditions being an obvious example) will hopefully lead to a process where education through access to information helps the organisers to facilitate the enjoyment of the overall experience of the event by eliminating some of the factors that would detract from this experience.

The extent to which this has already taken place at some events was one of the more surprising findings resulting from the audience samples that were taken at the Fields of Rock concert in Nijmegen in June 2005. A surprisingly large proportion of the audience admitted to having consulted the event web-site in order to obtain information on a variety of issues: transport facilities and weather forecasts comprising some of the prominent factors. It is clear that research into the demographic profile at concerts linked to how concert issues were communicated to the audience helped to identify how important electronic media is today as a marketing tool. From electronic communication it is clear that access to the area was made remarkably smooth and the audience were clearly aware of the transport links and facilities that were provided.

The other major element of research that the Nijmegen concert focused on was the system of measuring the pressures on the front row of the audience generated by the crowd pushing on the safety barriers at the front of the stage. The measurements were obtained by the system of pressure sensors installed in the barrier (BLMS system) that had been pioneered by Patrick Jordan, managing director of Mojo Barriers. The process is described in Chapter 5 and the findings are contrasted with those obtained at the Rosklide Festival where the barrier system at the front of stage is one that the organisers of the festival have developed as a unique means of controlling the crowd migrations in a festival environment, particularly one where there is a variety in the type of artist that is participating. By supporting the readings from the pressure barrier with synchronised data taken from participants wearing heart rate monitors and by video camera footage of the sections of the crowd nearest the stage, this aspect of the research has the potential to help determine how to make the safest possible environment for large outdoor concert arenas, as well helping to identify some of the more extreme physical extremes that lead to injuries both external and internal.

In chapter 4 one of the assessments produced by the first year of students on the Foundation Degree Course can be found. The student was Mark Hamilton, the managing director of Rocks Steady Security & Crowd Safety Company. It comprises the safety plan for a large concert at the Milton Keynes Bowl, one of the exercises required in order to complete the Foundation Degree Course in Crowd Safety and Management. As an exercise it provides a template for the preparation of a crowd management plan for a large-scale event. As such, it is the perfect illustration of how far the industry has developed in terms of the concern and the detail that is undertaken in the preparation for the management of major events. It is an illustration of the progress that has been made in protecting the safety of the public who attend events in what is one of Britain's growth industries in the entertainment sector. The success of the rest of the research programmes that are detailed in the other chapters and in the rest of the work undertaken in the Centre for Crowd Management and Security Studies will be measured by the extent to which they are able to add anything further to the procedures and controls that the industry already uses and that are illustrated in Mark Hamilton's project.

Chapter 5 reveals the results of the pilot project on barrier pressure which identified a number of issues which have then been incorporated into the final project the results of which are to be published in 2008. This project has been commented on both favourably and unfavourably by those in the industry and owing to its high profile a great many of what would otherwise have been unassailable obstacles have been discussed and developed to create a worthwhile piece of work. It must be remembered that this work is a preliminary work and that many of its conclusions have needed further work to clarify their position in the overall scheme of the project.

The final chapter is a distillation of a series of notes taken at the Popkom health and safety seminars in Berlin in 2006. These seminars enabled the construction of a series of pan-European safety issues discussed by festival promoters from throughout Europe. Although many of the major promoters and organisers were not present, this chapter still gives an interesting focus on generic and specific pan-European issues.

1 CASE STUDY OF MONSTERS OF ROCK EVENT AT DONNINGTON PARK 1988

Abstract

On 28th August1988, two young men died and a third was seriously injured in a fatal crowd-related incident during an open air rock concert billed as the *Monsters of Rock* at the Donington Park motor race circuit in north-west Leicestershire. This paper is a personal account of my involvement in what is now commonly referred to as the Donington Disaster.

Introduction

My involvement at the *Monsters of Rock* was as Head of Security, and as such I was employed by Aimcarve, the company responsible for promoting the event. I attended all pre-meetings and I had a good working knowledge of the site having worked on all events since 1980. At the 1988 event I was responsible for all security issues which included crowd control and the implementation of crisis management strategies should the need arise.

At the time of the event (1988) there was no established practice to set up an Emergency Liaison Team (ELT) therefore this event did not have one. The police attended all Safety Advisory Group (SAG) planning meetings for the event but no police officers were present within the concert arena during the event. The police were fully aware of what was taking place during the event via radio communication but they did not take an active part in containing any of what turned out to be three separate incidents that took place or the subsequent rescue operation of the injured. The rescue actions were entirely undertaken by a team from ShowSec International Limited supported by St. John Ambulance.

The following account is not claimed to be a factual minute by minute account of what happened on that day, it is simply the recollections of one who was actually there. As with all accidents or incidents there will doubtless be other witness accounts from people who were present that day and will recall things differently. This is natural when people see things from different perspectives. My version of the disaster is however based on a broad view of the sequence of events and the benefit of radio reports to me from trained supervisors. From this wide perspective I believe my version to be an accurate account of the events that lead to the loss of two lives, the serious injury to one person and a traumatic experience for many other people who were involved either as victims or rescuers.

The incident at the 1988 *Monsters of Rock* concert has been the subject of much discussion by those that have an interest in crowd safety matters. At the time of the incident the media showed a natural interest, as would be expected when two people die in such high profile circumstances. Unfortunately, much of what was reported by the press as the cause and effect of the incident was inaccurate. For example, the name of the act quoted in some reports as being on stage at the time was the singer David Lee Roth when it was in fact Guns 'n' Roses. Other reports indicated that a high crowd density build triggered the incident directly at the front of the stage subsequently causing crushing. This was also inaccurate. Several other papers claimed that the group on stage refused to stop playing, and this was also inaccurate. Yet another report claimed that police were directly involved within the crowd at the time of the incident when in fact the police were not in the arena at all.

Confusion over what actually happened was perhaps due to the fact that there had in fact been *three* separate incidents that day and reporters were possibly unaware of this when they questioned people. Perhaps, confused by the different versions given by some witnesses, they (the press) simply cobbled together a version of a single incident. While this version may have satisfied newspaper editors it did little to help students of crowd safety to discover the true course of events. This account might therefore help those that have an interest in crowd safety to understand what happened on the 28th of August 1988 at the *Monsters of Rock*.

Previous History of the Event

Promoter Maurice Jones, Chairman of Aimcarve Ltd, the organisers, first staged the *Monsters of Rock* in 1980. Jones enjoyed a well-earned reputation for promoting good rock shows. The 1980 show was an immediate success with rock fans, many of whom travelled from different parts of Europe to be there. The demand for an annual rock show was clearly evident and the show has continued to be held annually.

Heavy rock groups came to regard the *Monsters of Rock* show as being a major international showcase, and to play at Donington was seen to be performing at *the* rock event in the heavy metal calendar. It was covered by virtually all the trade press, and in addition to being broadcast live on radio bands often filmed their performances for future video promotion to enhance a sales campaign of their latest recording.

Many fans travelled great distances to be at the event, regardless of who was performing as the headline act. At the first concert in 1980 the demand for tickets was such that people arrived and set up camp on the Monday prior to Saturday's concert. Over the years the promoter had actively discouraged camping and tried to present the event as a one-day concert not a festival. Nevertheless, some fans still arrived with tents on the Friday evening. The promoter did provide facilities for these people including toilets, lighting, large marquees (for those without tents), food vendors and vast amounts of firewood.

The campsite itself was an amazing prelude to a rock concert. Nobody appeared to want to sleep. There was perhaps what could only be described kindly as a *carnival atmosphere*. Rock fans have a well deserved reputation for a love of alcohol and giving them the opportunity to spend all night in a field with a ready supply of beer while listening to ear splitting rock music appears to be their vision of heaven. In fact some of them are known to have enjoyed the night on the campsite so much that they slept through the entire day of the concert and went home on the Sunday having had a wonderful time!

The Venue

Donington Park is a motor race circuit situated approximately mid-way between Nottingham and Derby at the village of Castle Donington. The site itself is next to the East Midlands International airport. The circuit has a long history of motor sport and the track has been upgraded to handle F1. However, it is perhaps best known as the home of the British Motor Cycle Grand Prix. Motor sport attracts large crowds and the venue had developed good working relationships with the emergency services. As one would expect, there is a major incident plan in place, which takes into account virtually any scenario that could occur at a motor sport venue situated next door to a major airport.

Structural security in terms of crowd management is good. A brick wall surrounds the track area and this is approximately 12 feet high and topped with barbed wire. Entry and exit gates are designed to cope with ingress and egress crowds in the region of 200,000 people. The concert arena area is situated in the inner circle of the track with a standing room area that can accommodate between 150,000 and 200,000 people. In practical terms however this number of people could pose problems with sight lines for a concert therefore attendance at the Monsters event would normally range from 50,000 to 100,000. Attendance for the 1988 event was given by the promoter as 85,000 people.

The stage was built at the north east corner of the arena, facing approximately south east so as to direct PA sound away from the village of Castle Donington and toward the open area of the airport. In 1988 the grass area immediately in front of the stage sloped down toward the stage at a gradient of approximately 1:20. At the time this was considered advantageous to viewing, however after the incident this area was laid flat.

The Police

As stated previously, I had been present at every Donington concert from 1980 and I have never seen a serious confrontation between the police and the fans. The police have always taken what I would describe as a realistic approach to the event. This is not to suggest that they ignored crime. Local officers have come to understand rock culture and realised that a torn denim or leather look of the average rock fan did not signify that they were a rioting mob. All police control vehicles, temporary police station and facilities were therefore positioned near the main entrance to the site and not in the arena.

Officers patrol the campsite during the evening and night of Friday but the event itself is left in the hands of a private security company employed by the promoter. The only officers in the arena in 1988 were two that were assigned as liaison officers and they were in the backstage area. In my opinion the working relationship between private security and all the emergency services prior to 1988 were good and since the incident they could be classed as excellent.

Pre-Planning

The event was licensed by the Northwest Leicestershire District Council who chaired regular meetings for some six months prior to the event. For me, planning for the 1988 concert began in March of that year with informal meetings with the promoter. At this point I was advised that Iron Maiden would be the headline act. This particular act had a long history of successful record sales and the indications were that they would attract a large crowd, but their stage act was unlikely to cause serious problems.

During the months leading up to the concert the local authority arranged a number of meetings that were attended by the emergency services, the promoter, St.John Ambulance, myself and Tony Ball, who at that time was my assistant and would act as the site controller on the show. At these meetings it became clear that an attendance of 85,000 people was likely. Accordingly, the promoter agreed to provide daylight vision screens each side of the stage to avoid crushing at the centre of the crowd. A single front of stage primary barrier constructed of scaffold and ply board was installed for the event. This design was common at the time. The event used only one stage.

On completion of a site survey I proposed that a total of 520 steward staff be deployed on the day and all parties agreed this number. In July we were advised that the line up of major artistes for the concert was to be:

Iron Maiden

Kiss

David Lee Roth

Guns 'n' Roses

I had worked previously with three of the four named acts and they were considered to be low risk in terms of crowd behaviour. However, the fourth act, Guns 'n Roses, were a new young American act that we knew little of. Our risk assessment indicated that their stage act was aggressive in style and that they had strong record sales that would possibly attract a large number of their own fans to the show. Our audience profile indicated that these fans would be younger and more volatile than we would normally expect. The term used to describe this new trend in heavy rock was *Thrash Metal*. This title was given to indicate the way that these fans thrashed about wildly to the music to a point where they appeared to be hitting each other. As a result of our risk analysis we increased the number of security staff in the front of stage pit to 40.

The Incident(s)

The weather conditions prior to the concert were bad: it rained continuously from the Monday to the Thursday. Nevertheless the crew completed construction of the site on time. By Friday the weather had improved but conditions were still very wet and it was necessary to impose restrictions on vehicle movement around the site. On Saturday, the day of the concert, the weather remained overcast with occasional showers.

The doors opened to the public at 0800hrs and ingress was completed without serious incident. Those fans that had arrived early made their way directly to the front of the stage where security were not able to sit them down due to the wet ground conditions. However the crowd was cheerful and friendly and appeared to be happy to wait until the supporting acts would start to appear. During the period of their wait recorded music provided by a disc jockey from BBC radio was played.

Incident #1

At 1300hrs the control room received a message from the supervisor backstage advising that high winds were causing a serious problem to the daylight screen position at stage right. A rigging crew was alerted and I arranged to meet with Tony Ball at that location to assess the situation. By the time that we reached the location however the complete screen assembly had collapsed and was only prevented from falling onto a section of the crowd by a steel fence that surrounded the backstage area.

The ShowSec supervisor had moved the crowd from the danger area and a rigging crew was attempting to retrieve the damaged screen rig. Efforts by the rigging crew were continuously frustrated at this time as a small section of the crowd insisted on attempting to stand underneath the suspended rig because the screen was still relaying live pictures of the act on stage. Their actions however put them in great danger. My actions at this point were to deploy more staff from the pit to secure the danger area, cut the power to the screen and secure the damaged screen so that it would not fall. It was not necessary to stop the show as the band on stage shortly finished their act. The team operation to retrieve the screen took approximately one hour but before it was finally completed Guns 'n' Roses went on stage. Almost immediately I received a report from the pit supervisor that there was an unusual high level of crowd activity taking place in front of the stage. At this point I detailed a security team to return to the pit. I remained at the screen location to ensure that it was safe and I detailed my assistant, Tony Ball, to go to the pit and send me a situation report.

Incident #2

At approximately 1415 hrs Tony called me on the radio and asked for me to come to the pit urgently. I immediately went to the area which was approximately 100 yards from where I was. On arrival at the pit I saw that there was a great deal of activity within the crowd. Density was clearly at 0.3 immediately in front of the barrier, however this was not a serious problem. At approximately ten rows back however a density of approximately 0.5 allowed room for lateral surges, which were becoming a problem. I witnessed continued lateral crowd surges that ran across the complete length of the front of the stage. One particular surge started at stage right and stopped suddenly with a crowd collapse at the centre of the audience approximately 15 yards out from the front of stage. It was immediately obvious that this was a serious situation as approximately 50 people were involved in a crowd collapse. I sent a four-man team into the crowd to assist and assess the problem. At the same time I sent a message to the stage to ask the singer with Guns 'n' Roses to stop the show as we had a problem. The singer immediately stopped the show and he then used the stage PA to calm the crowd and advise them of the problem.

The advance team reached the spot and attempted to send back a radio message but unfortunately their communications failed due to the fact that victims of the incident grabbed at their radios and pulled the microphone lead out. At this point the team leader signalled to me to go to the spot. I instructed Tony Ball to remain in charge of the pit and I advised the control room, which was now managed by my business partner Gerry Slater, that I was going out into the crowd with another team. The show was still stopped at this point.

On reaching the spot I found that the advance team was dealing with approximately 10/15 people that had obviously been at the bottom of a crowd collapse. Ground conditions were bad and the people involved were covered in mud, and I decided that they should all be extracted from the crowd for their own safety. We managed to lift most people up and were passing them toward the pit when unfortunately the band on stage assumed that the incident had been fully contained and they resumed playing. Suddenly, the whole crowd around us erupted. A large section of the crowd, and two of our own security team, collapsed in front of us. I witnessed approximately 30/35 bodies that suddenly piled up in front of me covered in mud. Our efforts to pull people off of the pile were hampered by the fact that people behind us climbed onto our backs in an attempt to what we now know to be crowd surfing. In some cases these people dived over our heads onto the pile of bodies.

At this point I lost communications, my radio and earpiece was ripped from me. I was not therefore able to advise Tony of the situation. He realised however that we were in serious trouble and he quickly dispatched another ten-man team to assist us. At the same time he stopped the show for the second time. Once assistance reached us I was able to establish a cordon around the scene and retrieve the bodies. Tony had managed to establish a line of security people that extended from the pit to us and this enabled us to pass people back to St. John Ambulance staff who were stationed at stage right. We managed to retrieve over 30 bodies, all were covered in mud, some were bleeding and others had obviously vomited. When we reached the bottom of the pile we discovered one person unconscious. This person was immediately passed to the pit where he was resuscitated by Steve Johnson, a ShowSec pit team member.

Unfortunately, as we removed what we took to be the last casualties we discovered another two bodies underneath them. These two were both laying face down in about four inches of mud and they were almost covered over. At first I did not realise that they were people. The pressure load on these two victims was such that we had to dig under them with our bare hands to turn them over. We managed to extract both of them from the mud but they appeared to us to be lifeless. Suddenly the band started to play again and crowd conditions made it impossible for us to examine them in any detail. We immediately evacuated the victims to St. John where they were removed to hospital but were found to be dead on arrival.

Two senior officers, having been advised by control of the incident, arrived at the scene. The first indications were that the police wanted to stop the concert. After further discussions with the promoter however the show was allowed to continue as the police then decided that no purpose would be served by stopping the event. It was agreed in fact there might be a risk to public order by doing so as the majority of the audience were not aware of the seriousness of the incident.

Incident #3

At 1700hrs David Lee Roth was on stage. Both Tony Ball and myself had remained in the pit area to monitor the crowd. There had been no further incidents since Guns 'n' Roses had finished their set but we had decided to remain in the area. At approximately 1715hrs I noticed a young woman stage right about ten yards out who appeared to faint. She disappeared from my view and she did not reappear. As I was the one that knew exactly where she was I advised the team that I was going in to find her. I went into the crowd and on arriving at the spot I found a young woman aged approximately 15, laying face down on the ground. The crowd parted and I was able to check her condition. She was still breathing, there was a pulse and there were no obvious signs of injury. As she would have been in danger where she was I lifted her up to take her back to the pit where medics could attended to her.

At this point the pit team signalled to the crowd to part to allow me room to bring her in and I started to do so.

As I approached the pit I noticed one member of the pit team begin to climb the front of the stage. I can only assume that he was in a state of shock from the earlier incident because he climbed onto the stage and pleaded with David Lee Roth to halt the show as there had been too many injuries and the show should be abandoned. The singer, not realising the fact that he was a member of the pit team, assumed he was about to be attacked and called his two personal bodyguards onto the stage. They promptly grabbed hold of our man and literally threw him off the stage into the pit. Some sections of the crowd that had realised what was happening took offence at this and a dynamic surge toward the stage occurred. It was possibly that this incident is the one that the press later mistakenly reported as being the point where Lee Roth refused to stop the show.

At this point I was still in the crowd with the young woman in my arms. A member of the crowd, presumably seeing my security shirt, then decided that all security staff should be attacked and he hit me in the face with a one-litre plastic beer bottle even though I was obviously carrying a casualty. Although the bottle was only half full he hit me with enough force to knock me sideways onto the ground. This happened near to the barrier and fortunately the pit team was able to grab the young woman and I suffered the indignity of being rescued by my own pit team. The team also managed to recover our shell-shocked security man, who had actually missed the pit and landed in the crowd. He was also taken to St. John medics where he later made a full recovery.

There were no further incidents. Iron Maiden completed their set and the show closed on time.

The Inquest

The inquest into the two deaths at Donington was held at Loughborough Town Hall during February 1989. After four days of listening to testimony from more than 30 people that were involved in the incident, the verdict reached was accidental death. The coroner praised the efforts by the pit team by saying *"their efforts undoubtedly saved lives"*. It was recommended that the following measures should be taken to prevent a similar disaster:

- Muddy conditions should be made less hazardous
- A person should be positioned on stage to have overall control of safety
- The giant stage should be moved so that it is not at the foot of a slope

It was also recommended that a working party be set up to discuss safety at concerts.

The Aftermath

The sense of shock resulting from the Donington disaster was the catalyst for a review of the Greater London Council (G.L.C.) guidance for pop concerts, which was current at the time. A review body chaired by Richard Limb from the Northwest Leicestershire District Council invited members of the concert promoters association, private security companies and volunteer groups to work with local authority officers and the emergency services throughout 1989/90 to formulate a new guidance document for concert events. The result was the *Guide to Health, Safety and Welfare at Pop Concerts and Similar Events*, perhaps more commonly referred to by the colour of its cover as *The Purple Guide*. The front cover had a photograph taken of a crowd at a later Monster of Rock concert. I was pleased to have had input into the document in the form of the chapter on crowd management.

The Purple Guide was also significant in that it advocated that an Emergency Liaison Team (ELT) should be established for each major concert event. The ELT should be made up from members of the emergency services, the local authority and the security team. The role of the ELT is to immediately take command if a serious incident occurred, the police officer present would then take charge of co-ordinating command and control, and evacuation if necessary. The system is now standard practice in the UK.

Conclusions

On a personal level I learnt a number of lessons from that day.
1 The importance of a good control room.
2 Good communications are essential.
3 Staff need firm leadership – casual staff might not cope with disaster.
4 All senior staff must have a very clear understanding of their role.
5 Someone must take action to stop the show quickly.
6 Staff at the scene can be affected by what they witness; they too might need care and attention.
7 Training is fundamental to safety management.

ABOVE ALL, CROWD MANAGEMENT IS A TEAM CONCEPT

2 A PRELIMINARY REPORT ON THE RED HOT CHILLI PEPPERS' CONCERT AT HYDE PARK, LONDON, 19th AND 20th JUNE 2004

Contents of this Chapter

Part 1
Crowd Build Up at the Event

Part 2
Flow Capacities and Observations

Part 3
Findings from the four questionnaires on Crowd Strategy and Perceptions

This Chapter and the picture showing the Hyde Park crowd from the air has been printed with kind permission of John Probyn from Live Nation.

Part I Crowd Build-Up at the Event

Metres	Barrier 1 (min,sec)		Barrier 2 (min,sec)	
	Stage Right	Stage Left	Stage Right	Stage Left
0	0.00	0.00	0.00	0.00
1	0.23	2.26	1.14	1.27
2	0.36	11.01	1.47	1.32
3	0.21		2.22	1.53
4	0.49		2.43	2.03
5	0.55		3.15	2.15
6	1.01		3.26	2.37
7	1.07		4.57	2.46
8	1.19		5.31	2.56
9	1.36		6.21	3.15
10	2.01		6.48	4.31
11	4.07		7.18	5.06
12	6.31		8.33	5.30
13	9.05		11.36	6.01
14	9.31		14.22	7.15
15	11.45		16.37	7.57
16	11.54		19.10	8.13
17	12.02			8.26
18	13.13			9.40
19				11.17
20				12.13

The build-up of the crowd after the opening of the gates.

The Secondary Barrier Build-Up

On opening gates 10/11/12 and 13 the crowd proceeded by the most direct route to the secondary barrier. The merchandising and bar area (D in diagram, page 31) centrally located in the arena however was off centre towards the left hand side. This meant that from gates 10/11 and 12 the most direct route to the secondary barrier was to the left when entering the gate. Thus more than two-thirds of the audience gravitated to the left hand side of the control tower at the secondary barrier. The other third of the audience reached the secondary barrier down the right hand side of the auditorium. This is borne out by the fill capacity figures.

It took only 50 seconds for the first audience members to reach the barrier on

View from Hyde Park gate showing the positioning of the merchandising stand.

the left hand side (E) after the gates had opened. However those on the right hand entry to the arena reached the barrier (F) after 1 minute and 11 seconds. The 16 metre fill mark was reached on the left hand side after 8 minutes and 13 seconds, whilst it was reached on the right hand side after 19 minutes and 10 seconds. This showed that the left hand side of the arena was filling up more than twice as fast as the right hand side.

The density of the crowd on the left hand side of the arena was more than that of the right hand side by approximately two persons per square metre and this was largely due to the greater concentration of attendees on that side of the arena. During the event, audience members were regularly pulled out of the left hand side whereas the right hand side audience members were relatively comfortable and few were lifted out of the audience. This is shown in the photograph above.

The audience fill at the barrier to the left for the first 8 metres was approximately 12 seconds per metre whilst on the right for the first 8 metres was approximately 40 seconds per metre. Both sides slowed, however the metre fill on the left was between approximately 30 seconds and 1 minute whilst on the right it was approximately 1 minute 20 seconds to 3 minutes. Once this difference in left and right fill totals had been highlighted to the organisers, steps were put in place to change the layout and alleviate the problem.

Crowd management researcher marking out metre lengths to measure the fill capacity and fill timing at the front-of-stage barrier.

The Golden Circle Area

Golden Circle attendees arriving through gate 19 entered the primary barrier enclosure from stage right. On arrival they congregated around the stage right area filling up on one side only. After 13 minutes and 13 seconds the primary barrier area stage right had filled to the 18 metre mark. However on stage left by 11 minutes and 01 seconds this area had only filled to the two metre mark. The stage left area did not fill up until the Chilli Peppers took the stage at 8.15pm.

Whilst the Chilli Peppers were on stage on stage right there was a general gap of 8 metres between the secondary barrier and the back of the audience and on stage left there was a gap of 33 metres between the secondary barrier and the audience. At this time the crowd had still not become even across the whole of the inner gold circle area.

The audience fill stage right at the front barrier was approximately 45 seconds per metre whereas at stage left it was 9 minutes per metre.

Build-Up at Crowd Barriers from Entry Gates in Hyde Park

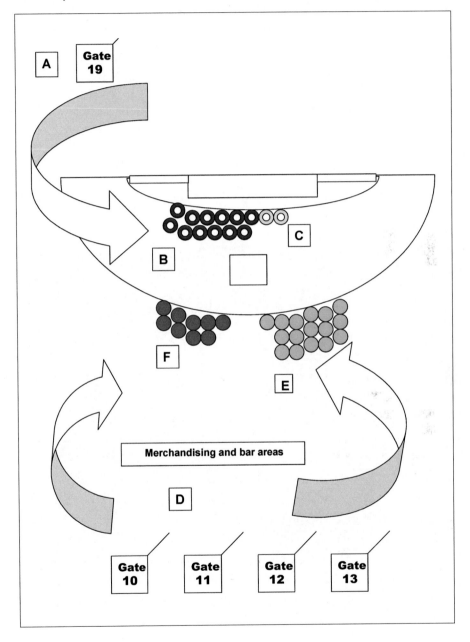

Conditions

The conditions were entirely different on the two days, which caused different reactions to the fill on both days. On day one the attendees in the golden circle encountered clouds of dust caused by individuals running to the front of stage barrier to gain the best views. However this did not stop their exuberance in reaching the barrier areas both in the golden Circle and in the rest of the auditorium. On the second day the downpour resulted in a very different scenario with driving rain accompanying the attendees into the auditorium. The wearing of macs and the soft and slippery ground hampered the progress of attendees to the two barriers.

The attitude of the attendees was different on both days and this can be picked up in the questionnaire findings. It is, however, clear that the organisers took all precautions necessary to assist the flow of attendees. Flooring was laid front of stage to stop dust rising and to keep the surface together if flooding occurred.

Audience members running into the golden circle area to gain a place at the front of the barrier for the Red Hot Chilli Peppers concert.

Part 2 Flow Capacities and Observations

The layout of the site for the Hyde Park concerts of the Red Hot Chilli Peppers was both unique and highly original. In effect, the organisers had created two separate arenas, one for the holders of the ordinary tickets and the other for the 'Golden Circle' ticket holders, who enjoyed sole access to the area directly in front of the stage and who also had their own, sealed off 'concessions city' with facilities that duplicated (with improvements in most cases) those available in the main arena for bars, food catering, merchandise, and toilets. The arena was in fact laid out so that there was little to differentiate the 'Golden Circle' from the main hospitality areas: unique ingress gates and the same preferential access to the front of stage area inside the secondary barrier. Where the hospitality areas differed was in the provision of marquees and (presumably) free food and drink.

In the opinion of the authors, the 'Golden Circle' tickets represented a huge addition to the value of the experience for these ticket buyers. Essentially, the Golden Circle ticket holders had the advantages of the experience and the atmosphere that a major outdoor concert brings, but with the comfort, the ease of access and the facilities enjoyed in most arenas. The additional benefit was that in almost every respect, the safety factors were also enhanced for not only the Golden Circle spectators, but also for the audience as a whole.

The main ingress gates for the arena were all situated at the far end of the arena from the stage which meant that on entering the auditorium, the ticket holders would pass through the entire site before they got to the front of the stage. The ingress gates for the Golden Circle tickets was situated at the opposite end of the site, adjacent to the press and the hospitality gates for the Record Company (WEA) and for the Press. Radio One hospitality and the main backstage entrance were at the same end of the arena, on the opposite side of the stage.

The four gates for general admittance were each divided into 15 lanes each, giving a total of 60 active lanes. The lanes were shorter than normal, at an average length of around 20 metres, but this allowed for the establishment of four main queuing areas and gave the early-comers a chance to relax in the queue outside of the very first arrivals who would have to maintain their position in the first half of the lanes in order to be first in once the doors opened.

Day One

Weather conditions on the Saturday June 19th were perfect for a concert. The sky was clear with the occasional cloud to provide cover from the sunshine. The temperature was about 25° centigrade and remained cool due to the constant breeze throughout the day. The crowd started to congregate at around midday, some three hours before the scheduled time for the doors to open.

The gates were opened at 15:32pm with the audience having been allowed into the lanes as far as the first search barrier some 10 metres in front of the main ticket check at the front of the gate. All 60 lanes were in use over the four gates.

Readings were taken at five minute intervals form all four gates, two lanes were selected at random from each gate, and then the output multiplied by 7.5 to give the total flow for the gate. Once the flow had reduced as the initial queues dispersed, the method changed to counting across all the lanes of each gate. As the dispersal of the initial queues that had formed prior to doors open took approximately 35 minutes, the figures used for the second reading at 16:30 pm were extrapolated backwards, rather than the initial readings on the first half hour taken forwards, again in the interests of accuracy.

After the first hour, the supervisors closed the first gate (10) of the four in order to allow the lanes to be cleared of the accumulated rubbish left from the initial rush, and to allow the staff manning the gate to take a break. This system was continued across the four gates so that after the first hour there were effectively three gates in use at any one time. It was noted that this in no way caused any build-up at the gates (beyond very minor temporary crowd surges) which presumably accompanied the arrival of tube trains at the Marble Arch station which was the nearest to the gates.

It was observed that the two outer gates registered more activity than the two inner ones, with Gate 10 being generally speaking the busiest gate throughout the period.

Day Two

The conditions on the Sunday were substantially different from those in place for the Saturday show. The temperature had dropped by at least 5 degrees centigrade and there was a stronger breeze. More significantly, there was the very visible threat of rain with heavy and menacing cloud cover.

The effect of this on the crowd at the front gate was that there were significantly less people queuing to get in as the doors opened. The make-up of the audience was different with less very young people in evidence and an older demographic in general evidence.

The doors opened promptly at 15:00. This time the main queues took just 20 minutes to clear the gates and the flow decreased substantially. The other major factor was that it started to rain very heavily almost as soon as the doors opened. Whilst the crowd that had gathered at the gates were anxious to pass through as soon as possible, the additional walk-up slowed almost completely until the rain stopped at around 15:45. It rained intermittently and heavily throughout the afternoon and the effect on the crowds accessing the gates was noticeable.

The effect of the weather was to slow the rate at which the crowd entered the arena and for the arena to take substantially longer to fill to its capacity. There was a natural and marked tendency for people to avoid entering the arena whilst heavy rain was falling and with ample facilities in the surrounding areas with the pubs and the restaurants on the Edgware Road all open and Oxford Street as a distraction, it meant that the ingress was staggered in a way that had not been noticeable on the previous day.

Observations On Ingress

The whole process was managed without incident and total control over the crowd and its behaviour was maintained at all times. Key factors were present in this were:

- Excellent and clear gate layout.
- Large number of lanes (60) available and a good rotation system of opening and closing gates.
- Good and solid lane construction.
- Excellent communication from staff to the crowd giving both information and instructions prior to door opening.
- Controlled movement on site due to the layout of the site with the merchandise tent dividing the crowd between the left and the right of the arena.
- Excellent deployment of crowd management staff in lines across the arena, to slow down the initial rush on the ingress.

Observations/Conclusions On Gate Ingress Data

The measurements taken over the two days enabled us to refine the means of data collection in concert arenas. The reality of this site layout is that it was so simple in conception and efficient in its operation that the task of monitoring the flows was made easier than we had previously experienced. The total number of lanes available and the fact that we could cover all of the ingress gates at any one time, meant that we believe we have achieved a greater degree of accuracy.

The cumulative figures given for the main arena ignore the capacity of the Golden Circle, which we were informed was 12,000.

On Day 2, we ran a parallel exercise at Gate 19 (the entrance for the Golden Circle) primarily as a control exercise.

The separation of the Golden Circle audience caused some problems with ticket holders trying to gain entrance through the main entrance gates, and having to be turned back though the full lanes because they could have no access to their part of the site through the main arena. This caused a very minimal disruption as the division of the two entrances was such that the degree of error leading any ticket holder to the opposite end of the site would have to be total.

The results are backed up by observations over the two days.

Overall, the degree of control and the excellence of the crowd management at these concerts, diminished the significance of the gate ingress data, whilst simultaneously allowing the research team the optimal conditions under which to refine the gathering of the data and the methods used in calculating the cumulative totals.

TIME	GATE 10	GATE 11	GATE 12	GATE 13	LANES MULTIPLE	FLOW PER HOUR	HOUR TOTAL	CUMULATIVE TOTAL	TIME OF ESTIMATED TOTAL	NOTES
15:30-16:00	613	539	571	617	7.5	17550	20475	20475	16.05	
16:30-16:45	1213	1126	1024	748	1	4111	18157	38632	16.45	
17:30-17:45	2174	1135	146	1191	1	4646	18584	57216	17.45	
18:30-18:45	1483	274	835	0	1	2592	10368	67584	18.45	

1 Formula for HOUR TOTAL in the first hour reflects the amount of time that the flow was at maximum for the initial queue to clear

2 Formula for HOUR TOTAL in the second hour is adjusted according to the above

OBSERVATIONS

1 Gate 13: 2 lanes closed at 15:45 for 10 mins.
Gate 10: 2 lanes closed for 10 mins

2 10 minutes of 4 gates, 5 minutes of 3 gates
Gate 10 closed after 9.5 mins

Concert Security Estimate of audience at 16:45 is 52,000

Day 1: Main Arena Gate Ingress Flows

TIME	GATE 10	GATE 11	GATE 12	GATE 13	LANES MULTIPLE	FLOW PER HOUR	HOUR TOTAL	CUMULATIVE TOTAL	TIME OF ESTIMATED TOTAL	NOTES
15:00-15:30	714	596	531	309	7.5	16125	12363	12363	16.05	
16:30-16:45	1183	1630	1636	886	1	5335	24630	36992	16.45	
17:30-17:45	1191	984	464	947	1	3586	14344	51336	17.45	
18:30-18:45	677	1228	0	864	1	2769	11076	62412	18.45	
19:30-19:45	0	352	0	619	1	971	3884	66296	19:45	

1   Formula for HOUR TOTAL in the first hour reflects the amount of time that the flow was at maximum for the initial queue to clear
2   Formula for HOUR TOTAL in the second hour is adjusted according to the above

OBSERVATIONS

1   Gate 13: 2 lanes closed at 15.45 for 10 mins.
    Gate 10: 2 lanes closed for 10 mins
2   10 minutes of 4 gates, 5minutes of 3 gates
    Gate 10 closed after 9.5 mins

Day 2: Main Arena Gate Ingress Flow

TIME	GATE	LANES MULTIPLE	FLOW	HOUR TOTAL	CULMULATIVE TOTAL	TIME OF ESTIMATED TOTAL	NOTES
15:00-15:40	664	4	2656	3541	3541	15:23	
16:30-16:45	607	1	607	2630	6172	16:45	
17:30:17-45	662	1	662	2648	8820	17:45	
18:30-18:45	515	1	515	2060	10880	18:45	
19:30-19:45	133	1	133	532	11412	19:45	

OBSERVATIONS

1   Initial queue cleared after approx 22 minutes.

2   First measurement taken over 40 mins

1   Formula for HOUR TOTAL in the first hour reflects the amount of time that the flow was at maximum for the initial queue to clear

2   Formula for HOUR TOTAL in the second hour is adjusted according to the above

Day 2: Golden Circle Gate Ingress

Part 3 Findings From the Four Questionnaires on Crowd Strategy and Perceptions

Questionnaire 1

The gender of those interviewed over the two days of the show was approximate ly 60% male and 40% female. The main age group interviewed on day one of the event was 16-20 followed by the 21-30 age group. On day two of the event the main age group questioned fell into the 21-30 age range followed by the 16-20 range. The groups sampled were random.

When analysing queuing at the gates, 66% of all of those interviewed on day one and 51% on day two stated that they were going to watch the concert from as close to the front of the auditorium as they could. The only other area where audience members were going to watch the concert from were in the centre of the auditorium: 19% on day one and 21% on day two. Although around the same number of attendees intended to go straight to the front of the stage on days one and two the audience was spread with less than half of those intending to watch the show from the front of stage heading in that direction on entering the park. Merchandising and the centre of the arena were also popular destinations.

On day one 77% of the audience perceived the queuing system to be either good or very good whilst on day two this dropped to 64%. Bearing in mind the differences in the climate over the two days this may have been an influencing factor. Only 8% on day one and 16% on day two felt that the queuing system was poor. The heavy rain on day two accounted for many of the negative responses as there was little cover and the downpour was heavy.

The information received prior to the event was perceived to be good or very good by 48% of the audience on day one and 47% on day two. 52% and 53% perceived that the information as OK, poor or very poor respectively.

The majority of those interviewed travelled to the concert by train, the second most popular method of travel was by car, and third by coach.

Traffic instructions were perceived to be good by 64% of attendees on day one but considered poor by 58% of attendees on day two. The directions from the coach park to Hyde Park were thought to be relatively poor with 51% of attendees on day one and 62% of attendees on day two perceiving that the directions were not adequate.

The queuing flow at the event was excellent with sufficient lanes for the crowd volume to pass through quickly. The majority of the crowd queued for less than thirty minutes, or less than one hour with only a small percentage queuing for over three hours. However, people in the latter two categories were recorded to have arrived well before the start of the show. The utilisation of the golden circle made queuing times less at these gates as the audience was guaranteed a place in front of the stage. Thus, the queues at the golden circle gate were relatively small compared with the rest of the show. However, it should be borne in mind that the golden circle only made up 8% of the total crowd capacity.

In the analysis of suitable/useful items brought by members of the audience to the event, on day one water was by far the most frequently required item with a coat coming a close second. However on day two 54% of the attendees had either a coat or a waterproof with water again being quite prevalent. This shows that the crowd for this event came well prepared for the weather although relatively few brought sunblock even on day one when temperatures were relatively high.

The majority of the audience utilised protective elements, showing that a large majority, from experience regularly attended concerts, were aware of the dangers of heat and cold during the day.

Questionnaire 2

The gender of those interviewed on day one inside the event was approximately 50% male and 50% female. On day two, there were slightly more males than females interviewed than on day one. However, the age range varied between the two days; on day two the majority of the attendees were in the 16-20 age group with a substantial number between 21-30. On day one however, the majority of those questioned were between 21-30, with 31-40 being the next most prominent age group.

On entering the event, on both days the most prominent area that attendees gravitated towards was the centre of the auditorium, closely followed on day two by the front stage area and other areas. On day one the centre of the arena was closely followed by the other areas and lastly by as close to the front as possible.

On day two 93% of the audience felt either safe or very safe inside the arena and the other 7% were indifferent identifying that no one questioned felt unsafe at the concert. On day one 95% felt either safe or very safe with only 3% feeling unsafe.

The majority of attendees (91% day one and 96% day two) made positive comments about the safety at the event. The attendees on day one identified a wider range of problems on day one than on day two. These are listed in the questionnaire responses.

On both days attendees felt that there should have been a wider range of services provided, but the main elements were waterproof capes, and waterproof sheeting, which could have been bought were felt to be the most important.

On day two 60% and on day one 44% of the attendees questioned in the arena were going to try and position themselves as close to the front as possible. The next most prominent place was in the centre of the auditorium. On day one the spread of the other options were more evenly distributed and these included the centre of the auditorium and on the rim.

On day one 70% of attendees perceived that they had brought the correct clothing for the weather. However on day two 51% perceived that they were unprepared for the rain on the day and had left without the correct clothing. However, the majority of attendees on both days were not interested in having information about what to wear.

The perception of the facilities on day one identified some interesting results. First aid scored the highest with 74% of those questioned rating it between 7 and 10. The sound quality scored 62%, the bars scored 54% between 7-10 on the satisfaction scale, toilets 45% and water provision 46%.

On day two, again, first aid and toilets scored highly on the satisfaction scale and sound quality scored 77%, possibly connected to the change in barometric pressure, heat and wind. However, on both days information scored quite low on the satisfaction scales netting 31% on day one and 42% on day two.

Questionnaire 3

The gender distribution on day one of questionnaire three was 58% male and 42% female. On day two it was 50.5% female and 49.5 male. The age distribution on the two days also differed in that, on day one the majority of attendees questioned were in the 21-30 age group with the 31-40 age group making up the second most frequently questioned group. On day two the 16-20 age group made up the majority of attendees questioned with the 21-30 age group coming a close second.

On day one 31% thought that the pit area was fun, 25% exciting, 21% sociable and 20% vital – only a small percentage thought it dangerous or antisocial. 83% had positive reactions to the pit area whereas only 14% had negative reactions.

On day two the picture was slightly different: 22% perceived the pit as a sociable area, 20% as vital and 19% as antisocial. Overall 68% identified positive connotations with the pit whilst 14% identified negatively with the area.

On day one 66% and on day two 7% of attendees questioned perceived that it was either important or vital to be at the front of the concert.

On day one of the event 84% of the audience questioned had not come up against the prohibition of crowd surfing or any regulations to calm audiences. On day two 74% had also not encountered these measures. When asked what their reaction would be to such measures on day one 29% were totally against any form of regulations, 19% would not attend concerts and 43% were understanding, relieved, pleased or indifferent that something was being considered to stop such behaviour in the pit.

On day two 34% of the audience questioned were totally against any form of regulation, 19% would not attend concerts if they could not crowd surf or mosh and 34% were understanding, relieved pleased or indifferent that something was being considered to stop such behaviour in the pit.

On day one 10% and on day two 18% of those questioned had been badly injured in the pit or front of stage area and this dissuaded 10% on day one and 30% on day two from entering the pit again. Those entering the pit again were only dissuaded usually for a few minutes from going back into the pit.

When identifying what would enhance the audiences' enjoyment most, if it were instituted: on day one special first aid assistance in the pit was the most common (although this was already provided). This was followed by special ventilation and drinking fountains at the front of stage, carefully trained security throughout the show arena, limited pit capacities and the banning of spikes, bags and other potentially dangerous items. On day two attendees favoured padded flooring and barriers and special ventilation and drinking fountains at the front of stage, closely followed by first aid assistance in the pit at all times.

Questionnaire 4

The gender distribution on day one of questionnaire four is 62% male and 38% female and on day two 50.5% male and 49.5 female. The age distribution on the two days was very similar and on both days the majority of attendees questioned were in the 16-20 age group with the 21-30 age group making up the second most frequently questioned group.

Very few attendees on either day classified crowd surfing as particularly anti social in a concert scenario. On day one fighting, queue jumping, urinating in public and attempting entry without a ticket were thought to be the most anti-social. On day two attempting entry without a ticket, fighting and urinating in public were also thought to be anti-social. Interestingly, bottle throwing was not considered an anti-social activity and not wearing a top was thought to be sociable by most.

When asked which of the activities people had taken part in at the concert on day one crowd surfing, not wearing a top, drinking heavily and pushing people in the mosh pit all featured heavily. On day two drinking heavily and crowd surfing were the main activities.

When asked which activities they regularly participated in during a concert on day one attendees responded mostly to crowd surfing, pushing in the mosh pit and drinking heavily. On day two drinking heavily was the most common followed by crowd surfing and then stage diving, not wearing a top and taking drugs.

On a scale of 1 to 5 on day one the most dangerous activities were classed as fighting, taking drugs, drinking heavily and pushing people in the mosh pit. On day two fighting, taking drugs, pushing people in the mosh pit and drinking heavily were identified as the most dangerous activities.

When asked how safe attendees felt it was safe to participate in such activities on day one the results were the same as for the previous question. However on day two although fighting was perceived to be the most dangerous to take part in, taking drugs and pushing people in the mosh pit were on a par with drinking heavily and stage diving.

Considering the safety of other attendees, on day one pushing people in the mosh pit was perceived as far the most dangerous activity to others. On day two fighting was perceived to be the most dangerous activity to others followed closely by pushing people in the mosh pit. Heavy drinking, taking drugs and stage diving were also thought to be dangerous to others.

On day one, when asked if any of the activities were stopped, whether it would lessen the attendee's enjoyment 71% felt that it would not. However on day two 47% of the attendees perceived that stopping the activities would mar their enjoyment.

On asking whether attendees perceived that safety was important to people at concerts, on day one 98% agreed with this statement. However, on day two only 82% agreed with the statement.

When asked if attendees felt that the concert environment was safe or unsafe only 3% on day one and 6% on day two perceived a concert scenario as dangerous.

Attendees were also asked whether they perceived that their behaviour at the concert may cause harm or loss of enjoyment to others, 12% on day one perceived that they would. However on day two 31% perceived that their behaviour may cause harm or loss of enjoyment to others.

Preliminary Conclusions

- The majority of attendees wish to watch the concert from the front of the auditorium.
- The queuing system employed at the event was though to be good. However, when it rained as cover was not available this tended to colour some of the attendees view of the queuing system.
- The information prior to the event was not thought to be particularly good. However as attendees did point out, Hyde Park is easy to find and there was information on the back of the tickets.
- The majority of people travelled by train to the event.
- Traffic instructions were variable and the directions from the coach park were poor.
- Queuing times were good and the number of lanes used was more than adequate for the event.
- The use of the golden circle was thought to be good.
- The crowd were relatively prepared for the weather at the event although less so on the second day.
- Most of the attendees were regular concert goers.
- Although many attendees identified that they wished to watch the concert from the front of the arena, many gravitated towards the centre when entering.
- A high percentage of the audience felt safe within the arena.
- The majority of attendees felt positive about the safety aspects of the event.
- Attendees felt that a wider range of free services should have been available e.g. a plastic sheet or a rain poncho.
- First aid was given the highest rating on both days as an identifiable service in the arena.
- The sound quality was perceived as good especially on day two.
- A high percentage of attendees had a positive reaction to the pit area
- Attendees perceived that it was vital or important to be at the front of the concert.
- Few attendees had come up against measures to stop crowd surfing.

- A relatively high percentage of the crowd were understanding about measures to curb crowd surfing.
- Many of the elements which could be introduced to enhance the attendees enjoyment were actually already in place.
- Crowd surfing is not classed as anti-social.
- Fighting is the activity which is most hated by attendees.
- Drinking heavily was perceived to be part and parcel of the event.
- Attendees perceived pushing in the mosh pit as the activity most dangerous to others.
- If harmful activities were stopped the majority of the crowd would not find their enjoyment lessened.
- The concert environment in Hyde Park was perceived to be extremely safe.
- Attendees are not aware that their behaviour affects others.

3

INVESTIGATION INTO THE STAGING OF VE DAY, TRAFALGAR SQUARE, SUNDAY 8th MAY 2005

PART 1: INTRODUCTION, AIMS & OBJECTIVES, METHODOLOGY

Erection of Herras fencing in Trafalgar Square.

Introduction

This report has been carried out at the request of Andy Ayres, managing director of Mantaplan, to provide an overview of the VE Day concert in Trafalgar Square. It is hoped the information and statistics contained within this report will assist the planning and production of future events in Trafalgar Square. Mantaplan propose that copies of this report will be distributed to the agencies and authorities who worked on the event. The area is well served by public transport with a mainline station (Charing Cross), and two underground stations in close proximity to the event arena, namely Charing Cross and Leicester Square. There are also excellent air and road links to the heart of the City of London.

The very nature and aspect of the site makes it a prime area for venue development, supported by the historical connotations of the area and the cultural, entertainment, hotel and catering infrastructure surrounding the site itself.

With a backdrop of the National Gallery, the site forms a natural amphitheatre enclosed on three sides ensuring particularly good acoustics for an outside venue. The area is also virtually self-contained and with a minimum of effort and disruption can be closed off to the public, traffic and services in a short period of time on a Sunday.

Utilisation of public transport and the lack of parking restrictions and the lifting of the congestion charge on a Sunday, means that car parking is not an issue. With the careful planning of a back stage area and the creation of easily accessible dropping off points it is clear that the access for artists, promoters, producers and services to the site does not cause a problem.

Owing to the excellent transportation links the site can be cleared well within 15 minutes and a fully serviced underground and over-ground facility can take people away from the site in a very short time.

Whilst fully understanding the need for more large venues in cities such as London, the main focus is on effectiveness and efficiency delivered by such a site in the context of the everyday business of a capital city and whether such events improve or reduce such effectiveness and efficiency. The crowd management and staff plan were both well set out, clear and comprehensive, identifying correct usage of existing standards.

The report centres on a number of areas and these are detailed below:

Ingress and Egress
Spatial Dynamics
Audience Questionnaire
Video evidence of pinch points and access egress problems

Aims & Objectives

In any report aims and objectives must be identified to ensure that there is some structure to the reporting mechanism. In this report the main focus lies in effective and efficient use of Trafalgar Square for music events. Thus the reviewed areas of ingress, egress, demographic information, travel preferences and migration are all vital to be able to triangulate evidence in the report. Thus the main aims for carrying out the research were as follows:

To ascertain the crowd flow into the venue.

To explore the egress pattern at the end of the show.

To identify whether the capacity rating of the venue was a fair reflection of crowd dynamics on the day.

To collect information on the crowd visiting the event.

To identify whether the transport infrastructure was sufficient to cope with an audience of this magnitude in the area identified.

To identify the possible benefits to the area from holding such an event.

Methodology

Introduction

The research utilised in this report is both qualitative and quantitative in nature, seeking to integrate and deliver evidence to support the findings of the report. The initial quantitative studies support the qualitative data and input from those involved in the event. Evidence used includes photographs, video evidence, questionnaires and participant observation. Triangulation of the data increases the validity of the findings.

Video Data Collection

The data collection was carried out utilising a number of methods. Firstly cameras were erected at the three entry gates at Duncannon Street, Cockspur Street and Northumberland Avenue. These cameras were focused on the crowd ingress at the three gates. The gates were opened at 17:00pm and the cameras were turned on by their operators at 16:55pm. Each camera was focused on their specific gate and these gates were filmed until each gate was shut. The Duncannon and Northumberland gates were closed at 19:00pm and the Cockspur gate continued to admit people until 19:45pm, at which time this camera was switched off.

During egress the three static cameras were again utilised plus three extra hand-held cameras were utilised to support the project findings. The hand-held cameras were used to film areas of interest around the venue. The first was employed above the mouth of the Underground station at the end of Duncannon Street. The second was employed inside the Northumberland Avenue exit as the main camera was focused on the other of the two exits in this area. The third hand-held camera was employed outside the Northumberland Avenue exit to identify the direction people were taking whilst exiting.

Questionnaires

A single questionnaire was distributed to 1000 attendees at the event, thus in a population of 15,000 results were taken on a 1:15 ratio. Taking into consideration that 1001 questionnaires were recently given out in a survey of a population of 60,000,000, this is an excellent return and this high level of response validates the results. Members of the team administered the questionnaires and this ensured that there were no spoiled responses. The questionnaires were administered in a random fashion with two team members deployed at each of the three entrances to enable the team to get equal responses from those coming from each direction.

From these questionnaires it was hoped to gain useful information about both demographics of the audience and their preferred means of and those travelling to the show.

The issues explored in the questionnaire were:

Sex and Age
Size of visiting groups
Travelling time
Mode of Transport
Where people had travelled from
Entry Gate used
Where people were going after the show
Reasons for coming to London other than the show

Ingress Flow Capacities

For ease of access and central administration capabilities Rock Steady, the security and crowd management company employed for the event were identified to feed back the number of people coming through each lane of each gate. This information was fed back to the Rock Steady headquarters where two of the project team members entered the numbers into a computer database. These were fed back to the team members at 20-minute intervals. As the event developed, this time sequence was increased up to a final count at a 45-minute interval. The counting process only stopped when all the gates had been closed.

Sample

The hand-administered questionnaires were targeted at those specifically attending the VE Day Event in Trafalgar Square and not those in the vicinity participating in other activities. The questionnaires were administered both outside and inside the gate. In total the sample of completed questionnaires represented the views of 1000 event attendees. Analysis of the questionnaires shows a spread across a wide geographic area but with a focus on Greater London and the surrounding area. Similarly the questionnaire also shows a bias toward female respondents, although it is clear from triangulated evidence that a 65:35 split between female and male is evident. A balance could not be maintained between age groups as the majority of those attending were within a narrow age bracket.

It is difficult to identify a simple typology for the other two areas of experimentation (video analysis and flow capacities), as they comprise random audience samples, which cannot be regulated.

PART 2: RESULTS OF THE QUESTIONNAIRE

Setting up the stage for the VE Day celebrations.

The foregoing demographic analysis of the audience at the event identifies that 65% of the attendees were female and 35% male. The age range of those attending the event is wide, ranging from 3 years to over 60 years in age. In percentage terms, 12% of attendees were over 60, 22% between 46 and 60, 17% between 35 and 45, 14% between 26 and 35 and 16% between 19 and 25. Thus 51% were in a category spanning between 35 and over 60, whilst 30% spanned an age group between 19 and 26. Only 14% of those attending spanned the age group 3 to 18. Overall 71% of the audience were over 25

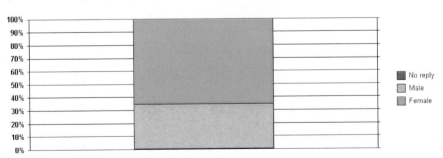

Figure 1: Sex.

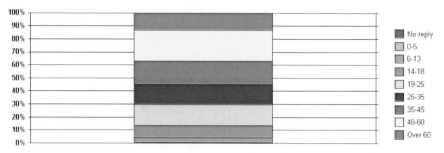

Figure 2: Age.

years of age. Linking the age to the sex demographic in figures 1 and 2, it is clear from the results that a large majority of the audience were female aged between 26 and over 60. A small number of attendees were male aged over the age of 60. This demographic reflects a number of possibilities.

- The age profile of the main part of the audience reflects those who remember the first VE day when they were young and were reliving the second.
- The over 60 male attendee includes a number of veterans who came to the celebration.

Picture showing the large number of female attendees queuing at Gate 2.

- The over 60 female numbers reflect those that were either widowed or had outlived their spouses.
- The artists utilised for this show although appealing to a wide audience appealed *en masse* to a more mature audience profile.

Both video and photographic evidence back-up the demographic evidence represented in this report. It is also clear from this evidence that very few small children were in attendance at the event and that pushchairs and prams were not very much in evidence on the day. Information from the London Ambulance Brigade also backs this up. Interestingly, the figures for trauma, and injury were very low with only two incidents reported on the day.

On soliciting responses both inside and outside the concert arena in relation to the size of group that people had come to the event within the following results were identified.

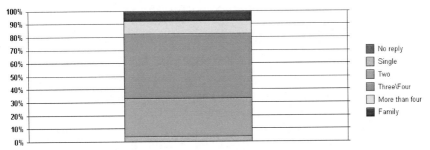

Figure 3: In what size group have you come to the event?

Just over 50% of the audience came in groups of three or four but only 6% came in family groups. 30% came in groups of two. Only 3% however attended the event by themselves. This is also supported by video and photographic evidence, where groups of three and four women are seen coming through all three gates and many of the couples were younger women escorting older persons to the event. It is possible that the specific nature of the event was not seen as a family event or one for single people but more of a group celebration. This is also possibly reflected in the artist line up.

It is clear from the following graph that the vast majority of the audience were only in the capital for the show and very few had other reasons for travelling to Trafalgar square.

87% of those coming to Trafalgar Square were there specifically for the show. Only 10% of those visiting the area also took part in other activities. These

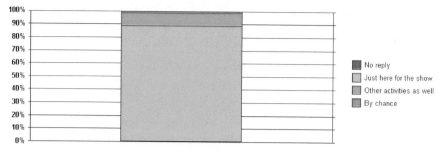

Figure 4: What is your reason for visiting this area today?

included visiting the National Gallery, eating out, visiting the National Portrait Gallery and other London attractions. This number must not be underestimated as the research identified in the region of 1500 people out of the audience taking part in other activities in Central London apart from the VE day event. A small number of people were just there by chance and had seen the show being set up. These people eventually entered the Cockspur gate when it was ascertained by the gate flow system that it was safe for them to do so. The event was free but tickets had to be ordered over the internet.

In figures 5 and 6 it can be ascertained that that the majority of people visiting the show came from a home base and would be travelling back home directly after the event.

In figure 5, 93% of people interviewed travelled to the show from home, 2% had stayed in a London hotel and 1% had travelled from friends. If this is coupled with the fact that over 80% of those interviewed came from the London area these figures are not surprising.

From figure 6, it can be seen that 81% of those attending the event were going straight home afterwards. However 12% were going on to an unspecified

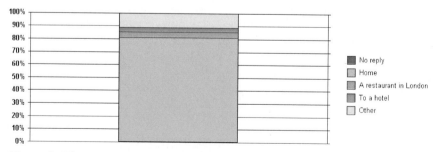

Figure 5: Where are you going after the show?

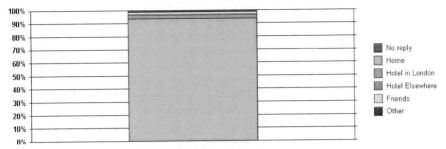

Figure 6: From where have you travelled today?

activity, 4% to a restaurant and 3% to a hotel. This is not surprising at the event took place on a Sunday and a large majority of people would have to be at work the following morning. This may have also restricted the number of people attending the show from further afield.

The mode of transport used to get to the event and the travelling time rather than distance were also explored. Figure 7 identifies the type of transport utilised.

32% of attendees had travelled by train, 31% by underground, 15% by bus 12% by car, 5% on foot and 1% by other modes of transport such as taxis. Many had travelled by one or more modes of transport and this has been factored into the calculations. Thus 83% had travelled by public transport or on foot and only 12% by private means of transport.

Figure 8 shows the travelling time from starting point to destination. 65% of those attending travelled for less than one hour. 27% for between 1 and 2 hours, 5% travelled for between 3 and 4 hours and 1% travelled for more than 4 hours.

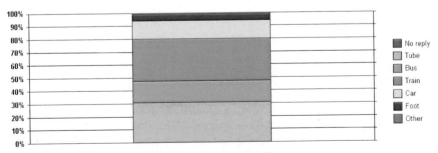

Figure 7: What modes of transport have you used?

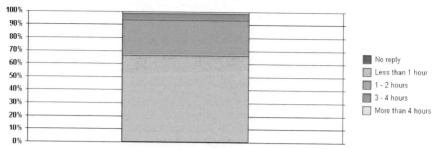

Figure 8: What was your travelling time?

The statistics show the following:

The majority of attendees came from the London area.

A large majority of those attending travelled from home.

A large majority of those attending were there specifically for the event and were travelling home afterwards.

A large majority of those attending travelled by public transport.

80% of the audience were in groups of 2, 3 and 4.

65% of the audience were female.

Other statistics not discussed in this report:

Up until 7pm 34.8% of the audience came through the Duncannon Street entrance, 49.5% through the Northumberland Avenue entrance and 15.7% through the Cockspur Street entrance.

Between 7 and 7.45pm only the Cockspur Street remained open and 6670 people came through this gate in a 45 minute period.

Thus 43% of the total audience entered between 7 and 7.45 pm through the Cockspur Street entrance.

The Northumberland Avenue Entrance.

The Duncannon Street Entrance.

The Cockspur Street Entrance.

PART 3: INGRESS AND EGRESS CALCULATIONS

Ambulance crew standing by at the entrance to Trafalgar Square.

Crowd Flow at Ingress

The methods for the measurement of the crowd flow at the ingress were based on the same spreadsheet that had been developed by the research team at previous outdoor events.

The main difference that the research team encountered at this event was that there were fewer ingress gates and fewer ingress lanes as well as a far smaller crowd capacity, which had a limit of 15,000. This enabled the team working on the project to produce far more detailed information relating to the counting process and results. It also enabled the facilitation of separate crowd clicker identification for every lane, allowing for a far greater accuracy in the flow rates recorded.

Preparation

The preparation for the ingress procedure was instituted at 14:00 hours when the crowd security company in charge of the event (Rock Steady Ltd.) initiated a sweep of the square to move those members of the general public who were within the bounds of the square. Until this point the square had been open access. In tandem with the sweep, the crossing points at the south side of the square were closed with fencing and barriers which were erected from Saint Martin's Place to the north edge of the church steps. This erection effectively sealed off the whole northeast side of the square. This sealing off process in the Square allowed for the ingress lanes to be erected at the respective gates, and to be manned, in anticipation of the end of the sound checks and the scheduled door opening time of 17:00.

The organisers had allowed for a total of 17 lanes, with six each at the Duncannon Street and the Northumberland Avenue entrances and a further five lanes erected at the Cockspur Road entrance.

During the build-up of the site, the early arrivals were held at a distance from the gates themselves, especially at the Duncannon Street entrance where they were held at the other end of the street at a barrier and only allowed access if they had a ticket or required access to buildings in the street beyond the barrier line. A separate barrier route to the north of Duncannon Street provided access to the Crypt Café and St. Martins in the Field. This procedure was not evident at the Northumberland Avenue entrance, where the spectators were gathered on the other side of a barrier as the lanes were being constructed.

The research team established the procedures for counting the data from the individual lane clickers, with the gate supervisors, and in particular with

Ingress and egress gates at Charing Cross.

Entry lane width as used for the VE Day celebrations.

the Control Room radio operators who would be instrumental in the timely gathering of the data, by taking readings over the air from the gate supervisors. The ability to carry out these readings in a timely and accurate manner were instrumental in the accuracy of the cumulative total figures for the audience numbers at any given stage of the ingress procedure.

Results

The figures taken from the clickers on each lane were relayed back to the Incident Control Centre at regular intervals and were then entered into a spreadsheet which calculated the total flow rates for each gate as well as the cumulative audience total showing the number of people that had entered into the arena at any given point of time.

These figures are shown in the table on the following page:

GATE/LANE TIME	DUNCANNON STREET						GATE TOTAL	NORTHUMBERLAND AVENUE						GATE TOTAL	COCKSPUR STREET					GATE TOTAL	TOTAL LANES IN USE	20 MINUTE TOTAL	AVERAGE FLOW PER LANE PER HOUR	CUMLATIVE TOTAL
	L1	L2	L3	L4	L5	L6		L1	L2	L3	L4	L5	L6		L1	L2	L3	L4	L5					
16:58 Gates open							0							0						0	0	0	0 HOUR	0
17:10	196	143	125	160	196	0	820	100	100	110	103	129	127	669	100	98	72	110	100	480	17	1,969	463	1,969
17:30	26	42	34	62	21	256	441	9	36	12	23	32	35	147	30	10	10	14	58	122	17	710	125	2,679
17:50	109	92	69	104	186	180	740	85	172	51	42	83	143	576	40	5	6	40	71	162	17	1,478	261	4,157
18:10	162	142	110	137	217	176	944	38	91	46	20	40	2	237	30	28	50	54	78	240	17	1,421	251	5,578
18:30	139	123	113	156	176	146	853	88	208	158	117	50	6	627	10	80	19	54	65	228	17	1,708	301	7,286
18:54	42	61	46	102	106	114	471	89	0	470	131	26	29	745	31	9	24	38	20	122	17	1,338	236	8,624
2 GATES CLOSED 19:15							0							0				80	0	80	2	80		8,704
FREE ENTRY 20:00							0							0	1838	3818	934			6590 n/a		6,590		15,294

Individual Lane Ingress Figures and Cumulative Audience Totals.

Observations

A number of observations were made from the figures, and these observations have direct implications on the successful running of similar events in Trafalgar Square.

1. Mode of Transport: The gate that was used most heavily by the audience was the Duncannon Street entrance. It would be normal to assume that this would be the chosen entrance for people arriving at Trafalgar Square by public transport and by train in particular, utilising Charing Cross Station as the point of arrival. The disproportionately heavy bias of people using the Duncannon Street entrance would suggest that the majority of people chose public transport as the means of getting to the concert; this is backed up by the questionnaire results which identify 83% of attendees travelling by public transport of by foot.

Similarly, it would be reasonable to assume that those members of the public that chose to travel to the concert by car would favour the Cockspur Street entrance as this is the entrance that is closest to the street parking that is available to the West of Trafalgar Square. In this area there are no parking restrictions and the area has no other usage due to the fact that the area is predominantly office accommodation. The conclusion arrived at through

Audience members entering Trafalgar Square through on of the main gates.

triangulation is that despite the lack of parking restrictions and the consequent availability of parking space, a disproportionate number of people chose to come to the concert by public transport.

2. Gates open time: It became clear soon after the security team had completed the 'sweep' of the public from Trafalgar Square, that the initial rush of public wanting to gain entrance as soon as the gates opened, was not going to be a problem as there was not a significant build-up of people at the gate barriers, in the period immediately before the public were admitted. It was observed that the demographic of the audience was probably the major contributory factor in this, as there was a notably lower proportion of teenagers in the audience than would be expected at many other outdoor music events with the exception of classical, MOR and concerts which attract a more mature audience.

Whether or not this was a function of the artist line-up, or whether this was caused by the very nature of the event that appealed to an older demographic, much of the behaviour that can put the audience at risk at the ingress was not observed. In particular, there was no great rush to the front of the stage barrier at the time that the gates opened, and that rush that did occur was easily contained.

Careful crowd management at the VE Day event at Trafalgar Square.

Crowd build-up at the VE Day event at Trafalgar Square.

The initial crowding at the front of stage barrier was orderly and controlled, and there was no evidence of any build-up of pressure on those closest to the front. The demographic is supported by the questionnaire results which identify that the main sex of the attendees was female and that they arrived in groups of 2,3 and 4 and that the average age of the attendees was 46.

3. Flow Rates: As has been noted, there was none of the large initial "surge" of people wanting to gain entrance to the arena as soon as the doors opened. As a result, the flow rate that was measured on the first reading that was obtained at 15 minutes after the gates had opened was substantially lower than was the norm for this type of musical event. The initial "rush" produced an hourly flow rate per lane of 463 in the first 15 minutes of the gates being opened, which is well below the capacity normally handled by the security teams given the number of lanes available. This also allowed for a ticket check procedure as well as a bag search. The flow rate then dipped, but began to increase considerably so that by 18:30 the flow rate was 65% of the initial rate recorded at the opening of the gates.

4. Cumulative audience figures: As a result, in the observed flow rates, it was no surprise that the figures for the cumulative audience totals were considerably lower than would normally be expected as the concert start time approached. It is important to remember that the tickets for the event were free and that they had been distributed to the audience by postal application through a dedicated ticket line. The tickets had all been allocated almost immediately, but as these were free it was not known whether the ticket holders would actually attend the event. This in fact became one of the salient features of the ingress procedure. At 18:54 hours, with just over an hour to go before the start of the main concert, the organisers had been able to establish that there were 8,600 people in the venue. At this stage, the flow of ticket-holders through the gates had been reduced to such an extent that a decision was taken to close the ingress gates at Duncannon Street and Northumberland Avenue, leaving only the gate at Cockspur Street open.

The organisers of the concert had anticipated the fact that the means by which the tickets had been distributed may have given rise to a situation where many of the tickets were not used. This was borne out by the number of people turning up to the gates on their own with six or seven tickets. As the tickets were free of charge, there was no reason for every individual not to apply for the full allocation of four tickets, even if these would not all be used. A second difficulty with the ticket distribution system was that a large number of people wishing to gain access to the show had been unable to obtain tickets through the application process. A large number of these people had travelled to Trafalgar Square in the hope of seeing the show. In addition to this, there were a significant number of people who had come to Trafalgar Square on the assumption that if a concert had been widely advertised as "free" it would mean that they would be able to gain free entry. In other words, they claimed not to realise that a ticket was necessary as a means of access to the event.

The possibility that the system of ticket allocation on a first come first served basis with no price barrier as a disincentive to purchase, may lead to a situation where only a small proportion of the ticket holders actually chose to attend the show, had not at first been anticipated by the concert organisers. However, owing to the fluid nature of such events it had been decided in advance that a meeting would be called at 18:30 with the Emergency Liaison Team, in order to review the attendance situation and to allow for the possibility of giving non-ticket holders access to the event arena.

In these circumstances, the figures provided by the periodic ticket counts were extremely useful, in particular the cumulative figure, which was relevant at the time that a decision needed to be made to allow more attendees into the event. From the chart, it is clear that the total number of people in the arena at the time of the meeting (18:30) was 7,286, or approximately half of the allocated capacity of the show. Additionally, the aggregate increase over the previous 20 minutes had not exceeded 2000 people, suggesting that the flow was steady and that there was little likelihood of a last minute surge of ticket holders.

Given this information, the decision was made to allow a controlled ingress of all non-ticket holders who wished to gain access to the venue. These people entered the event arena, along with the few last remaining ticket holders who had still to arrive. The implementation of this decision allowed the concert to begin with the stipulated audience capacity. A final count of spectators taken at just after 20:00 identified an estimated cumulative total of slightly more than 15,000 spectators in the venue.

This procedure was carried out utilising only three lanes of the gate at Cockspur Street. Each lane had security personnel present at the end of the lanes in order to present some form of natural barrier thus reducing the speed of the flow through the lanes, making it more controlled.

The security personnel on each of the three lanes maintained the click count for the whole period of this final phase of the ingress which lasted until the gates were finally closed at just after 20:00. The measurement cannot hope to be as accurate as the earlier counts owing to the mass influx of attendees in a very short period, but it is estimated that more than 6500 people entered at this time.

The research team was filming the ingress and the film of this procedure shows a continued but controlled flow of people into the arena throughout this 45-minute period.

The Use of Ingress Gates as a Means of Controlling the Distribution of the Audience in this Area

The decision to direct all new spectators in through the Cockspur Street entrance came about as a result of the fact that the organisers of the show had observed that the bulk of the audience had gathered at the South Africa House side of the square and that there was a great deal of empty space on the Canada House side of the square. As identified in the ingress flow data, the majority of the public had accessed the square through the Duncannon Street and the Northumberland Avenue entrances and that this, along with the fact that the audience who had gained access through Northumberland Avenue entrance, had not tended to look for the empty spaces as they entered into the square (see space diagram). The uneven distribution of the audience was clearly visible from the stage area and large gaps were noticeable on the arena floor. This uneven distribution was perceived to be a potential crowd safety problem and thus the decision to allow access only through the Cockspur Street. This rectified the uneven distribution of the crowd in the square by the time the concert began.

The other factor involved in this decision was the simultaneous need to accommodate the non-ticket holders that had gathered by the entrance gates. The most efficient means of controlling this sudden access (unhampered by checks) was clearly to direct the bulk of the additional ticket holders into the empty spaces. In the event that the area became overcrowded, then the process of allowing additional spectators in could quickly and easily be stopped.

PART 4: DIAGRAMS SHOWING THE SPACE

Crowds in Trafalgar Square during the event.

Definition of Trafalgar Square

The capacity rating for the event was in the region of 15,000 people in the area cordoned off in Trafalgar Square. However evidence collected on the day of the event identified that the area could in fact take more attendees than first envisaged owing to the migration patterns of the crowd.

The majority of the attendees migrated towards the front of stage area with this section the first to fill. As this area became saturated other attendees gravitated towards three other areas all of which had a seating option attached. The first was around the fountains area, the second on the upper wall both stage right and stage left of the square and thirdly the lower inner wall both stage right and stage left. The other obvious advantage of these three areas is that by sitting upon or standing on the seat or walled areas, including the fountain, the attendee gained a better vantage point when the show started but was able to find some comfort before the show began as the vantage point also offered a seated option.

Site Map One shows all access and egress points as well as key areas of interest. Site Map Two shows the way in which the audience approached the layout of the event. The purple areas are where the crowd took up positions in the Square and the green areas denote areas of space inside the site area. From spatial calculations there is about 66-75% of the space utilised by attendees at the concert; the other 25-34% is clear space. Thus the final total of 15,295 could be increased safely to just over 19,000 taking a 25% figure and to 21,500 taking a 34% figure.

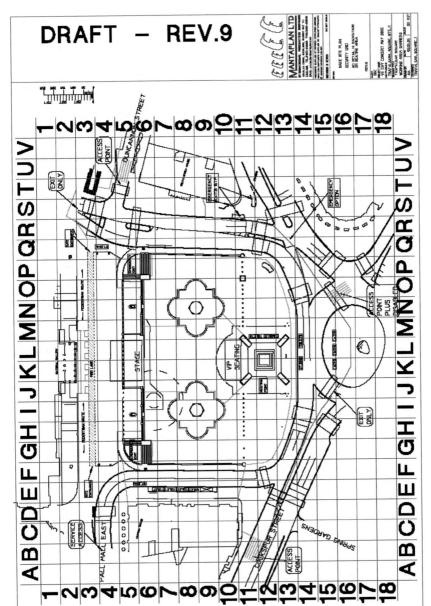

Site Map One.

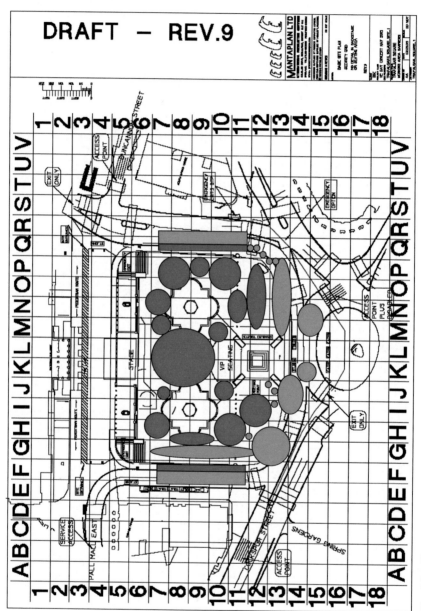

Site Map Two.

PART 5 OBSERVATIONS FROM PRE EVENT CHECKS AND MINICAM RECORDINGS

Introduction

During pre-event observations, the ingress and egress routes were measured to ascertain the evacuation capacity in relation to the site and crowd. There were two emergency exits of 4m width equalling 8m on Pall Mall East. However when the barriers were taken out this width increased to 16m. The Duncannon Street exit width was 19m, the Northumberland Avenue exit width was 12m and the Cockspur exit width was 8m.

Measurements were taken at the narrowest point and took into account furniture restrictions. The route from Trafalgar Square North toward Leicester Square was not measured as St John Ambulance crews used this area for vehicle parking and a treatment centre. This area was observed during egress and was found not to be used by pedestrians.

Thus the total possible exit width available at the time of measurement was 47m. Although this exit meterage was sufficient for both normal and emergency egress, it became clear during egress that restrictions were caused at both the Duncannon Street and Northumberland Avenue exits (explained later in egress flow) which could have caused serious crowd safety problems at an event with a less peaceful audience or where a different genre of music was in evidence.

During ingress three cameras were used on each of the entrances and the whole of the ingress until 7.45pm when all gates were closed was monitored and the footage viewed for this report.

Ingress

The arrival and ingress rate at the VE Day Celebration Concert was very different in nature to a mass arrival at a rock and pop concert at a greenfield site. Ingress and arrival were staggered and extremely slow. A number of reasons for this slow arrival and ingress can be hypothesised. Firstly the area where the event was taking place is served with a wide range of communication networks and thus arrival at an early stage on the day is not necessary. Secondly, the concert broadcast time was well known as was the gate opening time, thus people tended to either gravitate towards the square from other attractions in the capital (10%) or they came from the London area (80%), therefore travelling time was not an issue. Thirdly, as a large percentage of the audience came from the London area, coupled with road closure and traffic congestion, they would be well aware of the travelling time from home into Trafalgar Square and would focus on this timing. This is supported by the fact that the vast majority (83%) travelled to the show by public transport or on foot and 65% of the audience lived less than an hour from the event site.

A physical count was carried out on all ingress lanes and a 20 persons per minute count was achieved on all ingress lanes. Ingress rate was measured by diverting groups of ten persons to one lane for a period of 30 seconds. Flow rates were supported by a computer count system.

The Event

The following issues were identified at the event:

- Access to the disabled area was blocked once a major part of the crowd were in situ in the square.

- The Security team and the emergency services appeared to operate independently as they were not on the same unit.

- The crowd manager did not have immediate access to police CCTV pictures of crowd activity; messages were passed by the Safety Officer. Tactical crowd management is therefore an issue that needs to be considered carefully at any future event in this area.

- The role of the Event Safety Officer needs clarification in terms of level of responsibility for crowd safety in conjunction with the company utilised to manage the crowd.

Egress

As well as the three static cameras focused on the main egress routes, three hand held cameras were utilised to capture footage of areas of tension. Information from four of those cameras have been utilised in this report.

Tape 1 Underground Entrance Minicam – Duncannon Street

At the final egress, stewards were all in position and the areas were lit by normal street lighting plus additional floodlighting which was adequate for the area concerned. This augmented street lighting on all of the other exits. The Underground station and subway entrance was open for egress and ingress during the event egress time.

The average crowd flow into the subway entrance during egress was 25-30 persons per minute. Peak flow into the entrance was approximately 100 persons per minute for four minutes. During the egress period there was a high level of cross-flow caused by persons egressing from Duncannon Street and people coming from the Strand area. No barriers were used in the egress route and these were stored during egress. Both Pizza Hut and the Tavern placed refuse sacks in the direct line of those in egress mode causing partial restriction on the egress route. Staff refused to remove the bags even though they were made aware that they were causing a blockage hazard. Stewards had to be placed in position to divert the crowd away from the refuse bag area. The Tavern refuse sacks were removed to one side enabling full usage of the egress route.

Tape 2 Minicam Facing North West

This egress route was not used.

Tape 3 Minicam Focusing on the Back Entrance to Cockspur Street

The exit gates here opened inward as this was the only practical way to ensure full gate egress area. The crowd outside the gate passing behind would not have enabled the gate to open outwards. Stewards opened an additional panel in this area as the exit width needed to be wider for the oncoming crowd. This worked well. Just before egress a coach attempted to enter this area but was turned back by the police. A small number of people tried to enter this gate against the egress flow.

Tape 4 Minicam Right Hand Side of the Northumberland Avenue Watching from Outside the Arena

A large crowd of approximately 2000-3000 people had gathered outside the Northumberland Avenue entrance to watch the show from the road. However, in egress from this area the crowd were allowed to stay in position causing severe egress flow problems at the end of the event. A number of people deliberately positioned themselves to slow down egress and these people were not moved on. At one stage the stewards also blocked the gate in an effort to make the egress flow smoother. However the supervisor soon realised the problem and removed the stewards from the centre of the gate opening.

General Points

Egress for 15,000 persons was achieved in 15 minutes. However, this was largely due to:

- The good nature of the crowd.
- The majority of people utilised public transport.
- Transport serviced this area particularly well.
- Most people were in groupings of 2, 3 and 4, therefore single movement was reduced.

However, at a pop or rock concert where the audience demographics would possibly differ and the audience make-up was also different the behaviour and attitude of the crowd would have to be taken into consideration particularly when planning exit routes and final exit points.

It is considered the overall view of the concert and its environs, planning and execution were good.

PART 6 CONCLUSIONS

Final stage set-up before gates open.

Conclusions

General

1. The ability to make use of the vast transport infrastructure and the ease of movement with which this afforded the general public, were clearly all enhanced by the fact that the event took place on a Sunday rather than a week-day or a Saturday. This was key to the effective running of the event. It can be assumed that the same factors would impact on an event held on a Bank Holiday, however the lack of disruption and the ease of travel for those who attended, could not be assumed for an event on any other day. In the same way, the lack of the daily influx of office commuters into the area facilitated minimal disruption to be caused by the arrangements made for the concert were also minimised. It should be noted that neither of these conclusions could be applied to an event planned for any other day, and that this would have to be subject to further empirical testing.

2. The vast majority of those attending the event had a relatively short journey to the concert, (92% travelled for less than 2 hours) which further

re-enforces the efficacy of the transport infrastructure and enhances the consumer satisfaction of an event that is staged in Trafalgar Square.

3. Even with the one-off nature of the event, it is noted that at least 10% (1500) of the audience took advantage of the location of the concert to take part in other activities that were available in Central London. This suggests that the concert is a natural means for the promotion of tourist activities in London to either people living in the capital or to those wishing to visit from further afield.

Ticket Distribution

1. The method by which the tickets were distributed to the members of the public for a concert where there was no intention to establish any income stream from audience access, needs further examination. The cumulative gate totals showed that at 19:15 when the vast majority of those ticket holders intending to enter the concert had already entered the arena at this time, there were only 8704 people in the arena. This means that only one in two people to whom the tickets had been distributed had chosen to use their tickets. This in turn suggests that people had applied for the full allocation of tickets, in the expectation that demand would exceed supply, without necessarily knowing whether they would attend in full. The lack of a price deterrent made this behaviour perfectly feasible.

2. The research team were also able to ascertain that there were a significant group of people that wished to attend the concert who had not been able to obtain a ticket for the event. These people had travelled to the site in the hope of being able to gain access to what had been widely publicised as being a 'free' concert. Some of these people claimed to be unaware of the need to obtain a ticket for entrance to the arena, in the assumption that 'free' equated to no restrictions to entrance.

3. The organisers of the concert were able to remedy the situation owing to their knowledge of the approximate numbers of people that had entered the arena at any one time. At the point at which it could be safely assumed that the majority of those who had been able to obtain tickets had already entered the arena and the organisers decided to allow a controlled flow of non-ticket holders into Trafalgar Square. This enabled the final capacity to equal approximately 15,000, the figure that had been intended by the event planners.

4. It must be stated however, that this situation is by no means ideal, and that the successful implementation of the strategy to allow free access after a certain time can be attributed to the demographic of the audience. It can in no way be assumed that this would work as successfully for a younger demographic where the audience was more determined to gain access to the show.

5. In conclusion, the means by which the access of a fixed number of people gain access to the show needs to be reviewed, as well as the means of publicising the show. Radio bulletins on the morning of the show, still announcing a 'free' concert, to which there were no further tickets available, could well have led to a difficult situation with an audience that was less well mannered and controlled.

Capacity

1. A study of the distribution of the audience around the arena space, both in the build-up to the concert, and once the whole of the audience had been accommodated, suggests that there is room for a further increase of 34% to 21,500 based on available floor space and allowing for the standard requirement of 0.5 square metres of space per person. Given the layout of the square and the existence of visual obstacles to the stage, this should be reduced to a 25% increase, or 19,000 people. It is our understanding that it was the view of the event producer in association with the council that having studied the crowd on site during the event, the future capacity for a similar audience profile on a similar site layout should be 20,000 to 24,000.

2. However, any increase of the capacity would need to be accompanied by a more efficient means of distributing the audience once they had entered the arena. The fact that the vast majority of people had travelled to the show by public transport, and that the entrance for them had been either through the gates at Duncannon Street or Northumberland Avenue, meant that the audience had tended to congregate on the east side of the square in numbers that were disproportionate with those that had either entered through the Cockspur Street entrance or that had migrated naturally once in the arena.

3. The organisers were able to control this discrepancy and balance the spread of the audience throughout the arena by closing the gates at Duncannon Street and Northumberland Avenue at the time when the decision was taken to allow the additional non-ticket holders access.

This guided attendees into the less populated areas of the arena. Other means of distribution include enhanced signage in the arena itself and an earlier controlled use of the Cockspur Street entrance, particularly for those members of the audience who had gravitated towards the Northumberland Avenue entrance.

Site Layout and Communications

1. The potential to increase the use of the various entrances to enhance the crowd management procedures as outlined above, could be greatly facilitated by the simple addition of crowd managers to circulate those attending the concert into areas where crowd density was perceived to be less.

2. It was noted that the event control room was particularly small and cramped for the amount of use that it was scheduled for. In many backstage areas there is of course the potential for extra space, however in the case of the backstage area in question this was not an option and the space was at a premium and its utilisation had to be carefully planned.

3. A control room at a raised position would provide a less distracting working environment and in addition would have made at least two of the ingress gates visible to the control room, an obvious benefit in the event of the need to deal with any incidents at either of the gates (Duncannon Street and to a lesser extent, Northumberland Avenue).

4. It was noted that a decision had been made not to have an ELT office in an elevated position, as would be the normal practice. An alternative means of improving the communications between the various parties would have been to find means by which the CCTV cameras that were installed in the Emergency Liaison Team Control Room could be shared with the Event Management Team control room.

5. A further observation concerns the communication with the businesses and the restaurants in the immediate vicinity and the need to explain to them that whilst they were obviously in a position to benefit from the influx of the audience into the area, they may have to alter their normal operations to accommodate an event in this area. An obvious example of problems in this area took place at the egress point on Duncannon Street where a funnel was created for a large proportion of the public leaving the arena with the intention of gaining access to the transport facilities at Charing Cross Station.

One of the restaurants on Duncannon Street chose to fill the pavement outside with refuse for collection just prior to and during the egress. This greatly reduced the width of the street and created a potentially dangerous series of obstacles for a fast flowing crowd.

6. There also appeared to be a certain lack of knowledge amongst some of the audience as to the nearest and most convenient Underground facilities, and which of the various entrances would be opened at the end of the concert. This type of communication could be greatly enhanced by using the tickets to relay the relevant information.

It is clear from this report that on a Sunday Trafalgar Square is eminently suitable for a concert of this type. The area is well serviced by public transport and road links and thus ingress to and egress from the area causes few issues. The impact on tourism for such events is manifold. It increases throughput into the centre of London whilst facilitating the usage of other attractions.

It is clear that the event was well run, well policed and well managed, although a central sharing of communications and CCTV would enable further secure and safe monitoring to take place.

The site had good acoustics and causes minimal disruption on Sunday. The demographic of the day however calls into question how many people would be willing to attend a similar concert in this venue. If a single artist or band were to perform as the only chance to see them on tour, then the influx of people and the associated issues may make such a show more complex to manage. However this of course would depend on a number of imponderables, including mode of ticket sale, cost of ticket, marketing and the management of the crowd.

4 A CROWD SAFETY MANAGEMENT PLAN FOR AN OUTDOOR ROCK CONCERT EVENT WITH AN ATTENDANCE OF 60,000 PERSONS

Photograph supplied by Philip Windsor, Milton Keynes Borough Council.

Contents of Chapter

I. Introduction

Purpose of the Plan

The scale of the concert, and the responsibilities for public safety generated as a result of its size, requires the close co-operation of the event organisers, contractors, emergency services and the local authority. This plan will therefore detail the crowd safety contractor's roles, responsibilities and actions to deliver a crowd management operation that ensures the safety of those attending.

Event Overview

The headline act is Green Day who are an American punk rock band consisting of Billie Joe Armstrong, Mike Dirnt (born Michael Pritchard), and Tr Cool (born Frank Edwin Wright III). The band is currently on a world tour to promote their new album 'American Idiot'.

The headline act will be supported by UK performers.

The UK section of the world tour, including this concert, is being organised by a well known and established concert promoter, whose details are as follows:

> Rock On International Ltd (ROI Ltd)
> 1 The Right Way
> Motown
> West Midlands
> Tel. 0121 2222 0102
> Fax: 0121 2222 0202
> E-mail: mail@roi.com

Venue access arrangements

- Public access to the concert will be by ticket only.
- Guests will require possession of a concert ticket and can access the hospitality area(s) specified by their level of accreditation.
- Working personnel will require possession of a pass and can access the area(s) specified by their level of accreditation.

Concert Day Schedule

Doors open – 12.00 (noon)
Show start – 2.30pm with the first supporting act.
Show ends – 10pm

Venue capacity and occupant space

The venue has a capacity of 60,000 people for this concert.

The occupant viewing space consists of a an unseated bowl-shaped arena, with a standing arrangement on a flat grass surface facing the stage and alternative standing on sloping grass surfaces that surround two-thirds of the bowl's inner circumference.

An existing internal road between the perimeter fence and the lip of the Bowl provides space for concessions stands and toilets, as well as the final exit gates.

Please refer to appendices D and E at the end of this Plan for pictorial diagrams of the National Bowl and its surrounds.

Audience Age and Activity Profile

The age range witnessed at previous Green Day concerts suggests that the age profile for this event will be predominantly between 14 years old and 35 years old.

The gender ratio will be split 70/30, male to female.

The behaviour profile is expected to be minimal in terms of conflict and crime, but audience activity will be very lively with significant incidences of crowd surfing and moshing in the area close to the primary and secondary barriers.

Safety Information

It is recognised that the potential for a major incident to develop at a well-managed event is low, however in a confined space with a large attendant capacity the consequences of such an incident are high.

A site survey was conducted on the 12th April 2005 and completed in accordance with guidance available within *The Event Safety Guide (1999)*.

Based on previous experience, taking into account good working practice and consulting published guidance and the relevant sections of legislation, the overall risk assessment for crowd safety at this event is medium.

This document should not be considered exclusive and is intended to complement any Event Safety and Contingency Plan, and risk assessment produced by ROI Ltd.

2. Budget

The budget for this event is contained within Appendix A of this plan.

Amendments to the budget may be necessary after the concert promoter has given due consideration of the recommendations on page 29.

3. Statement of Intent

This Statement of Intent details the responsibilities agreed between RSES Ltd (the company) and ROI Ltd (the promoter) for the Green Day concert (the event) to be held at the National Bowl, Watling Street V4, Milton Keynes (the venue).

The company has agreed (please see the flowchart on next page) to provide a *crowd safety management service* for the event. Crowd management is defined here to be:

The systematic planning for and supervision of, orderly movement and assembly of people. Crowd management involves the assessment of people handling capabilities of a space prior to its use. It includes evaluation of projected levels of occupancy, adequacy of means of ingress and egress, processing procedures such as ticket collection, and expected types of group behaviour.

This also includes the provision of security staff licensed by the Security Industry Authority to undertake *'licensable activities'*.

An operational plan has been drawn up for the event and submitted to the local authority for approval and to other interested parties.

The terms of reference used are:

The Event Safety Guide 1999

BSi standard BS8406

Health and Safety at Work Act 1975

Private Security Industry Act 2001

Signed...
M Hamilton

For and on behalf of: RSES Ltd

Date: 25 April 2005

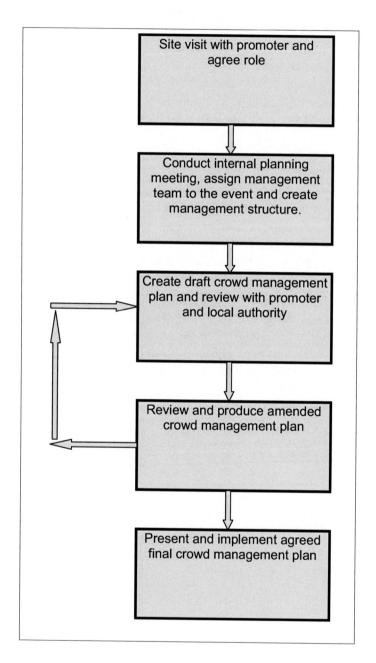

Site visit with promoter and agree role

Conduct internal planning meeting, assign management team to the event and create management structure.

Create draft crowd management plan and review with promoter and local authority

Review and produce amended crowd management plan

Present and implement agreed final crowd management plan

Event Planning Strategy
Equal Opportunities Policy

RSES Ltd is committed to providing equal opportunities in employment and service. This means that all job applicants, employees and members of the public will receive equal treatment regardless of sex, marital status, race, colour, ethnic origins, nationality or disability.

RSES Ltd values its employees, customers and the general public, and has a responsibility to promote good practices, which ensure their fair treatment and well-being.

FORMS OF DISCRIMINATION

The following are examples of the kinds of discrimination, which are against RSES policy:

1. Direct discrimination, where a person is less favourably treated because of sex, race or disability.
2. Indirect discrimination, where a requirement or condition, which cannot be justified, is applied equally to all groups but has a disproportionately adverse effect on one particular group.
3. Victimisation, where someone is treated less favourably than others.

POLICY STATEMENT

Any complaints regarding discrimination, direct or indirect, on grounds of sex, race or disability will be thoroughly, sympathetically and quickly investigated by RSES Limited. Any employee of RSES Limited who is found to have contravened this policy by carrying out a discriminatory act or acts will find themselves subject to the Company's disciplinary procedure.

Everyone within RSES Ltd has a responsibility to ensure that they conduct themselves in a way, which does not discriminate against any other employee or customer.

4. Management Structure – (Command and Control)

The concert promoter, ROI Ltd, has appointed one of its directors to maintain executive authority over the event.

Crowd management for the event will be conducted under the following structure:

Command Level	Grade
Strategic command	RSES Operations Director
Tactical command and designated **Crowd Manager**	RSES Senior Operations Manager
Tactical / Operational and second in command	Assistant Operations Manager
Operational command	Senior Supervisors and Supervisors

Please note the management structure flow chart on the page 13.

An RSES senior supervisor will be appointed to the Emergency Liaison Team, who will be joined by the promoter's representative and others from the police, emergency services, local authority and traffic management contractor. In the event of a major incident this group will convene at the Emergency Liaison Office, where a decision will then be made to transfer authority to the Event Commander from the police for the duration of the incident (see *appendix B* for the *Procedure for Transfer of Site Control to the Police*). The reasons and timing of this decision will be recorded in the event log, once authority has been handed over, all production and event resources will be at the disposal of the police.

During the normal course of the event, operational decisions will be made by supervisors under the direction of the Crowd Manager (Senior Operations Manager) stationed in Event Control.

Operational instructions will be transmitted by Event Control to supervisors, stewards and licensed security personnel. The standard operating procedures will be explained during the staff briefing prior to the event and thereafter in accordance with their duty instructions (*Appendix C*) and Emergency Evacuation Instructions.

Operational amendments, contingency development and further information will be relayed by Event Control to personnel throughout the site when necessary.

Management Structure

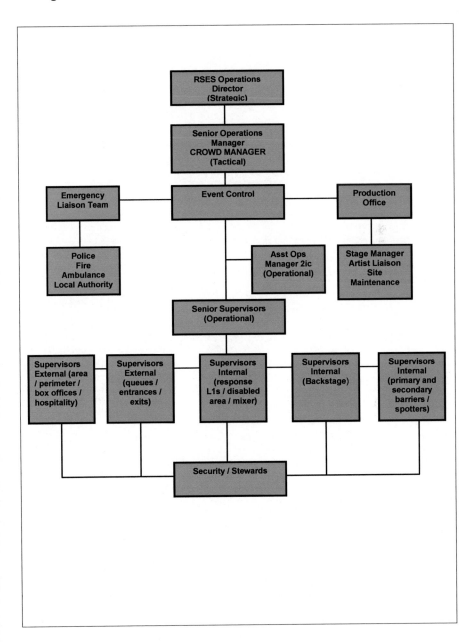

Deployment – Build Period

Location	Grade	Number	Start	Finish	Date
Site	L1	2	22.00	10.00	Mon 1st
Site	L1	2	22.00	10.00	Tue 2nd
Site and production	L1	4	10.00	22.00	Wed 3rd
	L1	2	22.00	10.00	
Site and production	L1	4	10.00	22.00	Thurs 4th
	L1	4	22.00	10.00	
Site and production	L1	8	10.00	22.00	Fri 5th
	L1	6	12.00	20.00	Backstage sound check
	L1	6	12.00	20.00	Front of House s/check
	L1	4	12.00	20.00	Artist entrance s/check
	L1	10	22.00	10.00	Overnight security

Deployment – Show Day

Location	Grade	Number	Start	Finish	Rdeployment
General Security	L1	10	09.00	12.00	
Traffic gates 1, 10 and Chaffron Way	U1	3	11.00	23.00	
Truck and bus parking	U1	4	11.00	23.00	
Emergency Access Gate 2	S1	1	11.00	23.00	

Location	Grade	Number	Start	Finish	Date
	U1	3	11.00	23.00	
Hospitality compound and marquee	S1	1	11.00	23.00	
	U1	8	11.00	23.00	
Response	L1	2	12.00	23.00	
Box offices x 2	U1	4	11.00	21.00	
Pedestrian routes	S1	4	11.00	23.00	
	U1	20	11.00	23.00	8 Redeployed to specific egress route locations
Queuing Lanes	S1	6	11.00	23.00	
	U1	36	11.00	23.00	
Entrance and exit Gate staff	S1	12	11.00	23.00	4 redeployed to primary and secondary barrier
	U1	36	11.00	23.00	8 redeployed to ramps and stairs to and from Bowl
	U1	36	11.00	23.00	Redeployed to primary and secondary barrier
Location	Grade	Number	Start	Finish	Date
Response	L1	12	12.00	23.00	6 redeployed to primary and secondary barrier
Primary barrier	S1	2	11.00	23.00	
	U1	14	11.00	23.00	Including spotters on stage left and right
Secondary barrier	S1	3	11.00	23.00	
	U1	30	11.00	23.00	Includes control duties into Pen
Backstage	S1	2	11.00	23.00	

	U1	16	11.00	23.00	
Response	L1	2	12.00	01.00	Dressing room cover
Stage access	U1	4	11.00	23.00	
Mixer	S1	1	11.00	23.00	
	U1	7	11.00	23.00	
Disabled Platform	S1	1	11.00	23.00	
	U1	5	11.00	23.00	
Medical posts	S1	1	11.00	23.00	
	U1	10	11.00	23.00	
Stairs and ramps to and from Bowl	S1	3	11.00	23.00	
	U1	12	11.00	23.00	
Response Teams x 4	S1	4	12.00	23.00	
	L1	16	12.00	23.00	
Perimeter fence (Grid ref E9 to H2)	S1	1	11.00	23.00	
	U1	11	11.00	23.00	
Perimeter Fence (Grid ref. K9 to I 2)	S1r	1	11.00	23.00	
	U1	11	11.00	23.00	
Site and production security	L1	10	23.00	10.00	

Management Team and Admin

Location	Grade	Number	Start	Finish	Date
All areas	M2 RSES Ops Director	1	11.00	23.00	
Event Control	M2 Senior Ops. Manager Crowd Manager	1	11.00	23.00	

Operational	M1 Asst.Ops Manager	1	11.00	23.00	
Operational sector management (Grid ref. A – H, 1 – 14)	M1 / Senior Supervisor	1	11.00	23.00	
Operational sector management (Grid ref. I – Q, 1 – 14)	M1 / Senior Supervisor	1	11.00	23.00	
Event Control	M1 / Senior Supervisor	1	11.00	23.00	
	S1	2	11.00	23.00	
Event Control call logging and relief	S1	2	11.00	23.00	
Emergency Liaison Team	S1	1	11.00	23.00	
Staff Welfare	S1	1	11.00	23.00	
Admin	S1	1	11.00	23.00	
	U1	2	11.00	23.00	

Total Number of Staff on Duty During Show

Grade	No. on duty
M2 – Senior Manager	2
M1 – Manager / Senior Supervisor	4
S1 – Supervisors	46
S1 Response team supervisors	4
L1 Response team	32
L1 general security – day	10
L1 general security – night	10
U1 – Steward	272
Total	380

Deployment – Break Down Period

Location	Grade	Number	Start	Finish	Date
Production and site	L1	4	10.00	22.00	Sun 7th
	L1	2	22.00	10.00	
Site	L1	2	10.00	22.00	Mon 8th
	L1	2	22.00	10.00	
Site	L1	2	10.00	22.00	Tues 9th

5. Staff Training

Crowd management employees are recruited and trained by:

> RSES Ltd
> 93 Constitution Street
> Edinburgh
> EH6 7AE
> Tel: 0131 554 4400
> Fax: 0131 554 3230
> E-mail: rocksteady@rocksteady.co.uk

RSES Ltd aims and objectives are: to provide a professional service through the deployment of trained, efficient and friendly staff; and deliver an effective service by maintaining an awareness of changes during the event and implementing improvements in safety, security and customer service issues.

Crowd management employees are trained to British Standard BS8406 (2003) and in accordance with the *Competency of Stewards* as detailed in The Event Safety Guide (1999).

- **Stewards** - have completed a formal training course in the following:
THE DUTIES OF A SAFETY STEWARD
- Appreciate the importance of the stewards role in crowd management
- Demonstrate flexibility and discretion in handling varied situations
- Code of Conduct
- Conditions of Employment
- Company Policies

THE EVENT SAFETY GUIDE (THE PURPLE GUIDE)
- Conduct and Competency of Stewards

HEALTH & SAFETY
- Health & Safety Requirements
- Risk Assessment Policy
- Your Responsibility
- Hazard or Risk

CUSTOMER CARE
- Customer Service Delivery
- Communication Skills
- Search procedures

Security Personnel – have successfully completed the stewards' basic training course and an SIA approved training course. They are also in possession of a licence authorising them to undertake *licensable activities*

Barrier and Pit Teams – personnel deployed in these locations have been especially selected and briefed to carry out a range of functions in regard to audience welfare, manual handling, conflict management, first response treatment and observation skills relating to types of crowd activity and signs of distress.

Supervisors – in addition to successfully completing all of the above, they have also demonstrated their skills on variety of events over a minimum two year period, gaining their promotion at the end of a six-month training course in both theoretical and practical crowd management techniques, including tactical communications and developed conflict management skills.

Senior Supervisors – have completed a minimum five years length of service are qualified trainers in all of the above and undergone tactical management skills development.

Managers – have demonstrated a wide range of abilities and tactical experience over a number of years during extensive operational experience leading to depth of knowledge in crowd management and safety issues further developed by qualifications, i.e. Foundation Degree in Crowd Safety Management (BCUC).

Risk Assessment – Members of the staff

This assessment is designed to assess the risk to the following:

It is the responsibility of the Senior Operations Manager to ensure that an on-going assessment take place throughout the duration of the event by individual supervisors. Any changes resulting in the escalation of either the severity or the probability rating of an identified hazard or the discovery of a new hazard are to be reported immediately.

Severity		Probability	
1	Minor Injury	1	Unlikely
2	Significant Injury	2	Possible
3	Serious Injury	3	Highly Possible
4	Major Injury	4	Probable
5	Major Incident/Fatality	5	Certainty

The probability and severity rating associated with each individual hazard is calculated before the controls are put into place. Once the controls are in place, the hazard and its severity may not change, but the probability will be reduced to a maximum of 'Possible'.

Risk Assessment Explanatory Notes

Severity Indices

1. Minor Injury

Abrasions, Bruising, Minor Burns (reddening of the skin).

2. Significant Injury

Lacerations leading to blood loss, Secondary Burns (leading to blistering), Sprains & Strains, Muscle & Ligament injury, Minor head injuries. Acute representations of underlying conditions i.e. Asthma, Epilepsy, Bronchitic Illness, and Diabetes. Hyper/hypothermia.

3. Serious Injury

Fractures, Trauma leading to significant blood loss, Head injuries leading to periods of unconsciousness. Acute representations of underlying conditions such as Angina.

4. Major Injury

Multiple fractures, Spinal or cervical injury, Multiple trauma, Injury affecting respiratory system, Head injuries leading to significant periods of unconsciousness. Myocardial Infarction, Status epilepticus/asthmaticus.

5. Major Incident/Fatality

Single or multiple fatality or large numbers of injuries in cat 3-4.

Risk x Probability Values

	1	2	3	4	5
1	1	2	3	4	5
2	2	4	6	8	10
3	3	6	9	12	15
4	4	8	12	16	20
5	5	10	15	20	25

Acceptable Risk   Risk

Acceptable with Adequate Control Measures

Unacceptable Risk

Area	Hazard source	Hazards	L	S	Risk	Control Measures	L	S	Risk
Exclusion Zones (Stage, protechnics storage, generator parking)	Fire from equipment	Burns Fire Explosions	5	3	15	Zone protected by suitable fencing. All non-essential personnel to be kept clear during operation of equipment. Stewards given instructions on the use of available fire extinguishers. Areas under constant supervision to ensure additional resources (Police, Fire Service and/or stewards) are deployed when required	5	1	5
External and Internal areas	Violence or disturbance from persons attempting to gain unauthorised entry	Manual handling Assault	5	4	20		4	3	12
	Movement of large numbers of people in limited space.	Crushing Tripping Public Order Crime	5	4	20	• Suitable and adequate number or crowd management personnel to be allocated to all areas. • Suitable barriers and fencing available to control access • Suitable and adequate emergency egress routes to be maintained. • All employees to be familiar with the layout of the venue, be competent in the task they are to perform, be aware of their responsibilities and know their means of reporting or summoning assistance • Crowd movement and condition to be monitored at all times from suitable vantage points. • All trip hazards to be isolated by event organisers. • Venue to be in good state of repair and free from hazards that may jeopardise the health, safety and welfare of others.	4	3	12

Location	Hazard	Risk	Severity	Likelihood	Risk Rating	Control Measures	Severity	Likelihood	Risk Rating
Primary and secondary barrier	Lifting	Manual Handling	4	4	16	Single person lifting is prohibited and lifting is done in teams of two or three	4	2	8
	Thrown objects	Personal Injuries	5	3	12	Awareness of objects thrown by the crowd into the area behind the barrier. Areas under constant supervision to ensure that lifting procedures are adhered to and monitoring of missile throwing is carried out. Communication with Stage Manager to make necessary preventative announcements to the crowd	5	2	10
Primary barrier	Noise	Hearing damage	5	4	20	Hearing protection notices posted and ear defender issue stations located around stage area	5	2	10
Backstage Area	Preventing unauthorised access	Assault	5	5	25	Key entry points double manned. Areas under constant supervision to ensure additional resources (Security and / or stewards) are deployed when required	5	2	10
Disabled Platform, and Mixer Platform	Unauthorised entry or climbing on temporary structures	Manual Handling	4	4	16	Areas protected with appropriate fencing and/or barrier. Access to compounds and platforms limited to authorised persons. Areas under constant supervision to ensure additional resources (stewards and / or Police) are deployed when required.	4	2	10
		Assault	5	3	15		5	2	10
		Crowd disturbance	4	4	16		4	2	10
First Aid compounds	Violence or disturbance from persons receiving treatment,	Manual handling / Assault	5	4	20	Areas protected with appropriate fencing and/or barrier. Access to compounds limited to authorised persons and public requiring treatment. Areas under constant supervision to ensure additional resources (Police and / or stewards) are deployed when required.	4	3	10

6. Event Risk Analysis Methodology

The EVA is based on one witnessed event and one reported event. These were two separate events held in similar surroundings and with an identical audience profile that relates to the concert covered by this Plan.

Balloch Park, Loch Lomond, 1996

The above venue hosted a two-day concert by Oasis at which three specific incidents arose.

Sound check day was on show day minus one and just prior to the band starting. One male local crew member was killed during an attempt to move a heavy goods vehicle that had become stuck in mud close to the secondary barrier. The emergency contingency plan was implemented and the site shut down temporarily whilst the police, and Health and Safety official attended the scene.

During the first night, the concert was temporarily suspended due to concerns about high levels of crowd activity including crowd surfing and moshing.

At the end of the first night a very serious near miss occurred when both the main lighting and emergency lighting failed on the principal exit route from the arena. Emergency contingency plans were implemented to divert large numbers of the audience towards alternative exits and routes out of the park.

Glasgow Green, Glasgow, 2001

This venue was host to the artist, Eminem and was subject to review by the licensing authority following a crowd related incident, which resulted in the temporary suspension of the concert. The focus of the post-event review concentrated on crowd management and barrier provisions in front of stage and also the delay between the show stop alert being made and the actual cessation of the performance. Details of the incident can be found on the BBC web site: http://news.bbc.co.uk/1/hi/scotland/1507811.stm.

Risk Assessment – Members of the Public

This assessment is designed to assess the risk to the following:

It is the responsibility of the Senior Operations Manager to ensure that an on-going assessment take place throughout the duration of the event by individual supervisors. Any changes resulting in the escalation of either the severity or the probability rating of an identified hazard or the discovery of a new hazard are to be reported immediately.

Severity	Probability		
1	Minor Injury	1	Unlikely
2	Significant Injury	2	Possible
3	Serious Injury	3	Highly Possible
4	Major Injury	4	Probable
5	Major Incident/Fatality	5	Certainty

The probability and severity rating associated with each individual hazard, is calculated before the controls are put into place. Once the controls are in place, the hazard and its severity may not change, but the probability will be reduced to a maximum of 'Possible'.

Risk Assessment Explanatory Notes

Severity Indices

1. Minor Injury

Abrasions, Bruising, Minor Burns (reddening of the skin).

2. Significant Injury

Lacerations leading to blood loss, Secondary Burns (leading to blistering), Sprains & Strains, Muscle & Ligament injury, Minor head injuries. Acute representations of underlying conditions i.e. Asthma, Epilepsy, Bronchitic Illness, and Diabetes. Hyper/hypothermia.

3. Serious Injury

Fractures, Trauma leading to significant blood loss, Head injuries leading to periods of unconsciousness. Acute representations of underlying conditions such as Angina.

4. Major Injury

Multiple fractures, Spinal or cervical injury, Multiple trauma, Injury affecting respiratory system, Head injuries leading to significant periods of unconsciousness. Myocardial Infarction, Status epilepticus/ asthmaticus.

5. Major Incident/Fatality

Single or multiple fatality or large numbers of injuries in cat 3-4.

Risk x Probability Values

	1	2	3	4	5
1	1	2	3	4	5
2	2	4	6	8	10
3	3	6	9	12	15
4	4	8	12	16	20
5	5	10	15	20	25

Acceptable Risk Risk

Acceptable with Adequate Control Measures

Unacceptable Risk

Location	Source / Activity	Hazard	L	S	Risk	Control measures	L	S	Risk
External/ Arena	Pedestrian routes audience Pressure	Overcrowding	4	4	16	Tactical deployment of sufficient stewarding resources along walkways, bridges and underpasses Implement diversion to alternative entrances	4	2	10
		Crushing	5	4	20		5	2	10
External/ Arena	Audience Activity Queuing	Crushing Trapping	5	5	25	Sufficient queuing lanes to ensure throughput. Lanes to be of construction to resist crown pressure Arena open in good time for audience access Signage to inform audience of preferred routes around the site Use of stewards to restrict access to congested areas Barriers and road closures to separate customers from traffic flows	5	1	5
Internal/ Arena	Arena Capacity	Overcrowding	4	3	12	Perimeter gates to control audience numbers Adequate area for numbers expected. Suitable primary and secondary barriers in place in front of stage Admission with ticket only Sufficient exits to allow for arena evacuation within a reasonable period. Perimeter fencing to segregate audience areas from public access Constant crowd monitoring by stewards, security staff and ELT Use of stewards to restrict access Gate closures if congestion develops Use of signage to redirect audience members CCTV crowd monitoring Pressure relief gates positioned to allow access to sterile area	4	1	4
		Crushing	5	3	15		5	1	5
		Tripping	3	4	12		3	1	3
		Crowd disturbance	4	3	12		4	1	4
Internal/ Arena	Audience Activity	Personal Injury from: Crowd surfing/ moshing	5	4	20	Installation of primary and secondary barriers to withstanding loading of 5kN per meter Constant crowd monitoring by a sufficient number of security and stewards deployed with the barrier system	4	3	10

Area	Activity	Hazard	L	S	Risk	Control Measures	L	S	Risk
Internal / Production area	Artist Areas	Presence of VIPs Crushing Hysteria Breach of secured area	5	3	15	All artist areas to be made secure and adequate numbers of security staff to be allocated. Artists to be isolated from public areas. All movement of artists to be monitored by backstage supervisor Artist liaison reps to fully inform security supervisor of artist movements	5	1	5
All areas egress	Normal pedestrian egress	Movement of large numbers of people leading to: Crushing Tripping	5	4	20	Movement of crowd to be monitored and managed by security and stewards Exit gates and pedestrian routes to be manned by stewards	5	2	10
		RTA	5	3	15	Implement pedestrian diversions Traffic management and police to manage traffic	5	2	10
Internal / Arena	Emergency Egress	Movement of large numbers of people under duress leading to: Crushing Tripping Public disorder	5	4	20	Sufficient exit width to allow site clearance in 8 minutes Emergency evacuation procedure to be put into action. All security, stewarding, crew and production staff to be aware of such procedures. Movement of crowd to be monitored and managed by security/crowd management teams. All evacuation routes to be manned and kept clear at all time. Suitable audience lighting to be made available and activated to assist with evacuation of areas during periods of darkness. Access to F/H and monitor engineer to be available to relay instructions regarding emergency announcements. Loudhailers available at strategic locations covering whole arena	5	2	10

Location	Hazard	Risk	L	S	Rating	Control Measures	L	S	Rating
Internal / Arena / emergency show stop	Large numbers of people becoming agititated and alarmed	Tripping Crushing Falls	5	4	20	Agreed showstop procedure ELT to assume control if required Implement contingency plan for show restart Sufficient lighting on audience viewing area Facility for PA announcements. Stewards to reassure cutomers with loudhailers and by direct contact Back up power for emergency PA	5	2	10
All Areas		Criminal/Terrorist Activity Leading to personal injury	5	3	15	Safety /security plans to be made available to local police. All areas to be checked for suspicious items prior to doors. All crowd activity to be monitored at all times. All unacceptable behaviour by members of the public to be dealt with accordingly. Bomb threats will be treated in accordance with attached instructions. Liaison with police to establish ongoing security state. Formal police ED search on show day.	5	1	5

7. Insurance

RSES Ltd are specifically insured to provide crowd management and security services, the details of which are as follows:

Insurance Broker:	Large & Co
	Any Street
	Any Town
	County Anywhere
Tel:	01234 567890
Contact:	Mr V Large
Principal insurer:	Lloyds Syndicate, London
Policy Number:	XYZ/0192837465/2005
Policy details:	Public Liability indemnity £5,000,000
	Employee Liability indemnity £10,000,000
Period of cover:	1st April 2005 – 31st March 2006

8. Survey Recommendations

A site survey was conducted on the 12th April 2005 and the following provisions have been recommended and agreed with the concert promoter, ROI Ltd.

1. It is recommended that the promoter gives serious consideration to the deployment of crowd management personnel on the night before show day and at the start of the morning. This will accommodate overnight queuing and oversee the build up of people arriving some time before the main deployment of security and stewarding personnel has been completed.

   It is estimated that seven personnel will be required for overnight queue duties from 22.00hrs until 10.00hrs in addition to the security detail who will be securing the arena.

   It is estimated that a further 24 personnel be deployed from 09.00hrs to direct and manage the expected early arrivals.

2. The box offices located at grid ref. K2 and F10 need to be relocated as the position currently planned will impede crowd flow at two of the busiest entrances.

3. The site visit uncovered large temporary gates and building debris blocking the main pedestrian walkway from the shuttle bus drop-off point to and from Gate 6, in addition to metal vehicle posts preventing vehicle access. All obstructions need to be removed to allow maximum use of the space and the area cleaned of debris to prevent injury.

4. There is an additional unmarked gate adjacent to Gate 4 and to achieve the final exit width required, it is recommended that the concessions stands marked for installation in this area are re-sited in another location.

5. The promoter will provide a grid map of the site that is acceptable to the police, emergency services, local authority and crowd manager.

6. A system of accreditation will be implemented for the duration of the concert, including site build-up, and break-down. Samples of both personnel and vehicles passes will be issued to the police emergency services and local authority.

7. Restricted areas, which require pass on entry have been agreed as the following:
   Stage
   Backstage
   Primary pit
   Secondary pit
   Mixer platform

8. Media access will be restricted to the primary pit and must be under escort at all times.

9. Emergency Liaison Office equipped to a standard acceptable with tables and chairs to accommodate all members of the ELT, and be equipped with mains power, lighting and four telephone lines to provide a suitable facility from which to direct responses to a major incident.

10. An Event Control room with suitable accommodation equipped with mains power, lighting, two telephone lines, three tables and chairs for six people to enable the efficient functioning of command and control.

11. A CCTV facility will be installed and a central monitoring station located adjacent to, or within Event Control. Coverage should principally be aimed at the entrances and front of stage area on the primary and secondary barrier and include auxiliary monitors in the Emergency Liaison Office.

12. Separate cash-in-transit security arrangements will be made and due notification given to the police.

13. Separate security arrangements will be provided for the concessions, merchandise and bar areas. Those responsible for this security provision will provide a point of contact to Event Control and they will be issued with the Emergency Evacuation Procedures.

14. A Primary Barrier and Secondary Barrier must be installed to assist with the distribution of crowd pressure towards the front of stage. This barrier must be the demountable type with a load bearing resistance of 5kN per metre run at a height of 1.2m.

> The barrier surrounding the stage thrust ("ego ramp") must not contain right angles corners that can result in sections of the crowd becoming trapped in pinch points.

> A working platform of a minimum of one metre wide running the whole length of the barrier will be required to enable security / stewards to safely extract members of the audience.

> To ensure that a working area is maintained at the secondary barrier, a second line of barrier will be erected to create a secondary wide pit.

> A mains water supply is required at the either end of the primary barrier and at three locations along the length of the secondary barrier. Suitable clean bulk water containers are required at each water point.

> The primary barrier will require a supply of 2500 disposable cups and the secondary barrier will require a supply of 5000 disposable cups.

> 20 water spray bottles will be required that will enable security / stewards to lightly spray water on those close to the barrier.

15. The area between the primary and secondary barrier will be know as the 'Pen' and access to this area will be on a first-come-first-served basis. The available viewing space has been set at 2000m², with a maximum viewing capacity of 4000 people.

16. A suitable lightweight demountable barrier system will be provided along with a site crew to complete the construction of queuing lanes.

17. Temporary lighting will be situated along all pedestrian routes within the arena where necessary and also in situ along routes leading to and from the arena towards car and coach parks, and public transport.

18. A cleaning company will be instructed to conduct regular sweeps of the queuing lanes to empty bins and remove debris to large refuse containers securely sited inside the Arena perimeter.

> Where access is achievable, cleaning crews will systematically remove litter debris from within the arena to prevent fire hazards, or wilful fire raising.

19. Vehicle curfew information is to be circulated to all site personnel and contractors to ensure that there is no unauthorised vehicle movement at a set time prior to doors open time and for a pre-determined period after the show has ended.

20. The event will follow standard practice for large concert events by utilising video screens to project a closer image of the concert to the wider audience to minimise crowd pressure on the secondary barrier.

21. A suitable wet and dry changing facility equipped with main power, lights, toilets and 50 chairs and six tables are provided for staff welfare and rest breaks.

9. Crowd Arrival

Doors open time is advertised as 12 noon.

The all-standing configuration of the Arena and audience profile suggests that there will be an early build-up at the entrances.

The venue location has been determined that means of arrival will be achieved as follows:

- Private transport (car and coach) 75%
- Public transport (bus and train) 25%

It is imperative that information is provided to customers in advance of their arrival to ensure they are suitably informed about parking arrangements depending on direction of and means of travel.

Sufficient and clear signs need to be located at critical road and pedestrian junctions and routes to ensure that the audience arrival is efficiently distributed around all the entrances to the Arena.

A public transport shuttle bus service will operate between the town centre and the drop-off point on Bleak Hall Industrial Estate.

Disabled parking will be situated in the West Car Park close to the disabled entrance at Gate 2.

It is estimated that 177 barriers x 2.5m will be required to complete the necessary lateral lanes and queue guidance system, which can be closely supervised to allow security/stewards to operate the requisite ticket and bag checks on people before they enter.

Crowd management arrangements have been recommended to accommodate the following crowd flow levels during the stages leading up to doors open time:

  Overnight   – slow
  06.00hrs until 08.00hrs – slow

08.00hrs until 11.00hrs – moderate

11.00hrs until 15.00hrs – heavy

An audience welfare provision including toilets, and refreshment outlets should be strategically located in agreed positions that do not impinge on crowd movement or affect crowd flow.

Queuing space on hard standing is available in the following locations:

Gate 1 – 550m²

Gate 3 – 1458m²

Gate 4 – 825m²

Gate 4 – 1020m² (auxiliary)

Gate 5 – 1160m²

Gate 6 – 1731m²

Gate 7 – 675m²

Total – 6744m²

It is anticipated that crowd density will peak between 12.00 and 14.00hrs.

Queuing will be maintained along hard standing paths, unless a part, or all, of the following contingency is required.

Note: Gate 3 – ticket and bag checks will occur before entry to the bridge, allowing this to be a free flowing section of the queue and not form a part of the static queuing area, which could lead to problems with dispersal in an emergency.

Gate 4 & 5 – Parking of coaches and production vehicles must be well planned and sympathetic to the space required for queuing in this area.

In the event that excessive numbers of people are present outside the site, the following contingency will be implemented:

- Consideration must be given to opening doors early to minimise the possibility of a crowd pressure build-up outside.

- Diversionary tactics will be implemented to ensure that underused space is fully utilised.

- The auxiliary gates adjacent to Gate 4 and 5 will be prepared in advance for use.

- The West Car Park may be shut down to create additional queuing areas for Gate 3 and control placed on access through the Chaffron Way underpass to prevent congestion inside the tunnel.

- Vehicular access via Gate 15 can be controlled, enabling staged pedestrian access towards Gate 4.

- Persons crossing the footbridge traversing Watling Street can be filtered to join either queue line towards Gates 1 and 7.
- Additional road space will be brought into use across the bridge traversing the A5 towards the Bleak Hall Industrial Estate.

The risk factor for the arrival phase of the event is medium.

10. Pre Doors Checks

A number of criteria need to be satisfied before doors can be opened to the public. Those established as underpinning elements to this process are as follows:

- The site manager has confirmed that all construction work has been completed and proclaimed the arena safe for public occupation.
- The adverse weather plan has been reviewed and any measures required to neutralise the effect of bad weather on the fabric of the arena are on standby or deployed.
- The promoter has been issued with the event licence by the local authority.
- The promoter is satisfied that the artist is on schedule to arrive at the venue.
- The protocol for all parties to agree that doors can open will be conducted in the ELT and the decision relayed to Event Control to notify all staff to proceed and allow the audience access.
- An acceptable level of security and stewards have reported for duty and are fully equipped and in uniform.
- Security/stewarding personnel for the entrances and exits have been fully briefed and deployed; entrance stewards are in possession of ticket stub collection bags; exit personnel are in radio communication with Event Control and confirmed all exits are unlocked and useable.
- Security/stewarding personnel for front of house have been fully briefed and deployed: including disabled platform, stairways and ramps leading into the arena, and sub-contractors on bars and concessions.
- Security/stewarding personnel for the restricted areas have been fully briefed and deployed and are in possession of the relevant pass sheets.
- Event Control has confirmed radio contact with all tactical and operational staff throughout the arena.

11. Ingress System and Entry Conditions

The audience will gain access to the arena by entering through the following gates:

- Gate 1 (4 lanes)
- Gate 3 (8 lanes in, 1 lane out)
- Gate 4 (5 lanes)
- Gate 5 (5 lanes)
- Gate 6 (8 lanes in, 1 lane out)
- Gate 7 (4 lanes)

Note: Vehicle Gate 10 leading to Arena Gate 2 will be used for emergency vehicle and artist access.

Gate 2 will also be used for disabled customers who will be escorted through the gate to ensure their safety and minimise the possibility of disruption to the movement of emergency or artist vehicles.

Each gate will be supervised by two supervisors commanding the following:

Each gate will have deployment of two licensed security personnel to deny entry to those deemed unsuitable.

Each lane will be manned by one bag/ticket checker and one ticket taker (a total of two staff).

To ensure that there is a maintained crowd flow: calculations have been based on an empirical study of pedestrian movement at a body eclipse of 550mm (unit width). In recognition of the bulky items carried by many members of the audience, entry lanes will be set at two unit widths (1.1m).

The number of 1.1m wide entrance lanes required has been calculated at a pedestrian speed of 20 people per lane per minute. The time taken for searches and ticket take has been accounted for. Flow rate therefore has been calculated at 1200 person per hour per lane.

The minimum number of lanes required are 20, however, in the interest of safety, 34 lanes will be installed. In the unlikely event that 60,000 people turn up at the same time, full ingress can be achieved within one hour and 30 minutes by the following calculation: 20 persons per minute x 34 lanes = 680 x 90 minutes = 61,200.

To ensure there is information on the number of people inside the venue, each gate will deploy staff to count manually those entering each lane. The numbers will be locally collated by the supervisor and recorded by them in their notebook. During the periods (see p. 34) of slow to moderate arrival, the supervisor will notify Event Control every 20 minutes of the number entering. During periods from moderate to heavy, the frequency of reports to Event Control will increase to every ten minutes.

Event Control will maintain an overview of entrance activity and when appropriate will instruct entrance supervisors to start the partial or complete conversion of entrances to exits.

In the event of a delay in opening doors or as a result of an entrance becoming inoperable, the following contingency will apply:

- Diversions will be implemented to direct people towards underused gates.
- Gate 5 (auxiliary) will be utilised and concessions restocking will cease until crowd flow has been restored to normal at the designated entrances.
- Stewards with loudhailers will announce regular updates on the reason for any delay and to reassure those queuing that action is being taken.

Method and Control of Artists, Guests and Production Staff Entry

Artists will enter via the designated 'Artist Entrance' at Gate 2 which is the closest point to access the back stage area.

Artist vehicles will be issued with a window pass that can be easily identified by police officers on road closure duty and security staff internally.

Tour and local production staff will wear an appropriate event pass and be allowed to enter by all specific entrances subject to the level of accreditation in their possession.

Sponsors and other guests will enter by Gate 3 on presentation of the appropriate invitation or pass.

Ingress System – Pen

Entry to the Pen will be on a first come basis and achieved by the accessing a corridor on either stage left or right.

The outer section of the corridors will be of the same technical dimensions of, and adjoining with, the secondary barrier.

The width of each corridor will meet the agreed exit times (section Egress on page 47).

Control of the corridors will be maintained by the use of three 1.1m lanes on stage left and right. Security/stewards will click count those entering until the capacity is reached. Thereafter capacity will be maintained by wrist-banding people as they leave so that they can re-enter.

Entry Conditions

The following conditions must be made known to the public in advance of their arrival. This is most appropriately conveyed by drawing attention to the details on the rear of the ticket, or as a wallet which is used to mail the tickets to recipients.

- Each person entering the arena must be in possession of a valid ticket; there will be no cash on entry for this concert.

- Ticket stubs will be retained exclusively in bags by security/stewards, so that a physical count can be conducted.

- Each person must be willing to subject their clothing and belongings to a search; anyone refusing to do so may be denied entry.

- Search protocols relating to equal gender. i.e. male to male, female to female, will apply.

- Items detailed as prohibited in the arena are as follows:
  - Bottles
  - Metal containers
  - Cameras and recording equipment
  - Alcohol and controlled drugs
  - Folding chairs
  - Fireworks
  - Offensive weapons
  - Any item deemed to be a threat to public safety

- There is no cloakroom or other storage area within the arena to accommodate items refused; customers need to be informed that the said items be taken back to their means of transport.

- There will be no pass-outs allowed.

There may be a need to relax the entry conditions, therefore the following contingencies will apply:

- Any person claiming to have an emergency, medical (diabetes) or physical reason (pregnancy etc.), for bringing in a prohibited item must be referred to a gate supervisor for clearance.

- In the event that there is unacceptable crowd build-up at the entrances, the search procedure may be changed to the selective method of searching those who are carrying large bags and/or wearing bulky clothes.

12. Event Monitoring – Method

The event will be monitored throughout by the Senior Operations Manager and a team of staff employed in the Event Control and CCTV Room.

Operating Alert State

It is intended to operate a three-tier alert system. On raising the alert state, the Senior Operations Manager will notify the ELT. When raising the alert state, the Event Control room should use the relevant internal code word to notify all radio holders.

It may be that the alert state need only be raised in a specific area i.e. Primary Barrier, a specific entrance or exit, or a grid referenced location. Should this be the case, the incident should be investigated by the relevant Senior Supervisor and a report then made to the ELT; a decision will then be made whether to broaden or raise the alert state.

The traffic light system of colour coding, GREEN, AMBER and RED, will be used to signify the current alert status as follows:

GREEN
Indicates that there is free flow both inside and outside the site, no build-up at the gates, no adverse weather conditions, all stewarding and medical resources in place and fully operational.

AMBER
Indicates unusually heavy pressure on gates, no free flow, areas of crowd density over 0.3 per m2 in large areas, site full to capacity, structural collapse or a bomb threat or suspicious package, localised outbreak of fire or crowd disorder; isolated patches of deep water or mud in high risk areas like gates, exit routes, etc. Medical or stewarding resources at only 60% effectiveness in high-risk areas or across the controlled area.

RED
This would be effective immediately where any amber state condition was confirmed by the Senior Operations Manager or on the advice of the Police that the initial problem indicated was becoming uncontrollable, or in the case of a confirmed threat such as fire, bomb, or structural collapse, widespread flooding, medical or stewarding resources at 25% of effectiveness.

The evacuation of the site would depend upon the area and the information available.

Radio Communications

A two-way radio system will be utilised. This will include two channels, each operating from two separate base stations with repeater capability.

The radio channels have been allocated as follows:

Channel One – Internal operations including barrier systems, backstage, production and front of house facilities and ELT.

Channel Two – External operations including entrances, exits and queuing areas.

A separate radio and channel will be employed in Event Control to maintain contact with the production office.

Two lap top computers will be time synchronised and used to transcript in summary fashion, all incoming and outgoing messages, the caller details and the action taken in response on each radio channel.

All hand-written notes taken during the event will be kept on file to support the computer log entries.

A large whiteboard will be installed in Event Control so that action messages can be viewed by all operators.

Large site plans and deployment schedules will be displayed inside Event Control for ready access to the required information during an incident or to direct redeployment.

Telephone Calls

Incoming calls will be recorded to retain information that may be required for corroboration within the computer logs.

Bomb threat telephone calls will be dealt with by the standard operating procedure as detailed on the Bomb Threat Checklist (appendix D).

Communicating general information or emergency messages to the crowd will be via the stage PA systems and stewards in possession of loudhailers distributed throughout the arena.

Response Teams

There will be four five-person response teams made up of four licensed security personnel (L1s) and one supervisor (S1) working internally and externally. They are tasked with conflict intervention, crime prevention and general assistance.

Reported Crime

Alleged crimes must be reported to the police. Anyone caught or suspected of committing a crime must be detained by licensed security personnel until the police arrive. This includes those found in possession of controlled drugs and/or offensive weapons.

In the event of a serious incident, the area involved will be treated as a crime scene and isolated from the public to preserve evidence until relieved by the police.

13. Crowd Final Egress

Due to the design of the National Bowl, the entrance and exits gates are one and the same therefore it is imperative that when crowd flow through the entrances diminishes, each gate is converted to an exit.

The fire authorities have advised that they require an emergency egress time of 15 minutes for full evacuation.

The method used to calculate pedestrian flow during egress is forty (40) persons per minute per unit width of 550mm.

Internally, the Bowl has five exit routes from the occupant viewing space as follows:

Stage left towards Gate 2	16m
Stage right towards Gate 3	16m
Ramps at rear of Bowl	24m
Total	56m

This will allow an egress time from the Bowl as follows:

Exit width 56,000mm ÷ 550mm = 101 unit widths x 40 = 4,040 persons per minute

4,040 persons x 15 minutes = 60,600 people

The Pen has a total exit width 8.8m providing sufficient exit width for persons to reach a place of safety within the following time.

Exit width 8,800mm ÷ 550mm = 16 unit widths x 40 = 640 persons per minute

640 persons x 8 minutes = 5120.

All tented structures and temporary buildings must be maintained within their certified capacity to achieve an evacuation time of three minutes as agreed with the fire authorities. Stairs and doors must be correctly signed as exits.

The evacuation of disabled persons from the disabled platform will be conducted by the stewarding personnel allocated to that area and with consideration of the need to prevent wheelchairs becoming caught in hazardous situations affecting both the disabled and able bodied.

The gates used for final egress at the end of the show are as follows:

- Gate 1 = 5.5m
- Gate 3 = 10.5m
- Gate 4 = 5.5m
- Gate 4 = 7m (auxiliary gate)
- Gate 5 = 5.5m
- Gate 5 = 5.5m (auxiliary gate)
- Gate 6 = 10.5m
- Gate 7 = 5m

Total final exit width = 55m

This will allow an egress time from the Bowl as follows:

Exit width 55,000mm ÷ 550mm = 100 unit widths x 40 = 4,000 persons per minute

4,000 persons per minute x 15 minutes = 60,000 people

Crowd management teams led by supervisors on radio will be required at all exit points, ramps and stairways from the Bowl, and to be placed externally at strategic junctions to monitor crowd flow and provide situation reports to Event Control.

Clear and well-lit signage is required to direct people towards car parks and public transport.

Close supervision to prevent congestion, crushing and/or conflict with vehicular movement will be required on four particular areas:
- Pedestrian footbridge across Watling Street
- Bridge at Gate 2
- Bridge at Gate 3
- Chaffron Way underpass
- Junction of road at Gate 14
- Coach parking bridge at Gate 15

Additional lighting will be required along the pathways and within the car parking areas to facilitate safe egress.

Under the direction of Event Control, a contingency plan to divert people will be implemented by the crowd management teams located at the critical junctions, in the event any one route becomes congested or blocked.

14. Emergency Action Plan

A full contingency plan has been prepared by the licensing authority, listing the roles and responsibilities of all agencies as well as significant locations and the actions to be undertaken by each organisation.

Responsibility for crowd management is under the direction of the Senior Operations Manager, assisted by a number of senior staff responsible for various areas. If a situation escalates to a full or part evacuation of the venue, all production crew will be advised by their supervisors as to the action to be taken. Specific attention should be drawn to the following:

Show Stop Procedure
There will be one spotter on stage right who will maintain a direct line of sight with the crowd within the Pen and at the secondary barrier. The spotters will be equipped with a headset and two-way radios to enable an exclusive line of communication with a Contact Supervisor within the primary and secondary barrier. They, and their replacements, must be introduced to the stage manager/sound engineer before they take up their post

If the spotter identifies a problem he/she will radio the Contact Supervisor who will assess the situation and decide what steps to take.

If the Contact Supervisor calls for the show to STOP then he/she can do one of two things:

a) Radio the spotter to stop the show; he/she will immediately inform the stage manager/sound engineer to stop the show.

b) If the Contact Supervisor is close enough, they can go directly on stage and instruct the stage manager/sound engineer to stop the show.

c) The show must be stopped immediately when called for.

The decision to se-start the show will be made after consultation with all parties concerned, including the ELT.

The show stop procedure has been developed to protect the safety of those in the crowd and beyond. Its use requires swift and decisive action, and when called for it cannot be overridden by anyone, including the promoter.

Termination of Power Supplies
The production manager will ensure that the main PA and lighting systems remain in operation until the audience has left the arena, before terminating supply. In the case of power failure leading to loss of the PA the Stage Manager should immediately notify the ELT.

Evacuation of Artist & VIPs
The evacuation of artists and VIPs and their entourage into a public area can

be a hazard in itself. The security team working in that area should handle movement of the artists to a safe place, to be determined depending on the nature and location of the incident.

Emergency Vehicles

In the event of an incident requiring the response of additional emergency services units other than those on duty within the site, the request must be directed through the ELT. All designated evacuation routes and roadways will be maintained by security teams under the direction of the Senior Operations Manager to allow access for emergency vehicles.

Pre-determined Messages

A number of pre-agreed announcements have been prepared for broadcast over the emergency PA and by loudhailers to aid crowd management. These messages will be dependent on the nature and seriousness of the incident, and only after consideration of the appropriateness and timing of any announcement.

Operational Action – MEDIUM ALERT

In the unlikely event that an emergency situation is declared, the Event Control supervisor will activate the following plan.

- Event Control will confirm with the ELT that they are aware of the situation.
- The control room supervisor will advise the Senior Operations Manager and Senior Supervisors.
- The respective Senior Supervisor will immediately go direct to the location as instructed by control and co-ordinate the incident.
- Assistant Operations Manager (2ic) will go direct to the ELT and co-ordinate the crowd management operation with the relevant authorities.
- All supervisors are to maintain radio silence until contacted by Event Control, unless they need to announce a localised Amber or Red alert.
- All other radio holders will maintain their present channels and await instructions from control.
- Event production office will be informed.
- All parties will be advised of the exact area of the threat by reference to a common grid map.

- All security/stewarding staff placed on evacuation standby as per standing instructions.
- All exit and entry gates are to prepare for evacuation of the site by arranging for all obstacles to be removed.
- Rendezvous point for emergency vehicles is to be staffed and secured.
- Where the incident is contained and condition LOW is declared, all parties will be advised using the stand-down code.
- Where the situation could become serious, a stand-by for condition HIGH will be issued.
- Supervisor in the Mixer Platform is to liaise with the Sound Engineer to ensure he can be contacted and on stand-by to receive instructions.
- Supervisor in the stage area is to liaise with the Monitor Engineer to ensure he can be contacted and on stand by to receive instructions.

Operational Action – HIGH ALERT

Where the incident is considered as very serious, the Senior Operations Manager will now receive instructions directly from the ELT and direct all security / stewarding staff to assist emergency services as requested, whilst the situation exists.

The Senior Operations Manager will immediately instruct the following:

- Declare alert state HIGH.
- All exit and entry gates to be cleared of any obstructions, i.e. barriers, queues, etc.
- Rendezvous point to be secured for emergency services, and emergency routes cleared, police assisted by security / stewards.
- Pedestrians will be directed away from the threat and the incident area secured.
- Show stop procedures will be implemented and the recovery or cancellation phase will be implemented by the ELT.

15. Evacuation procedures

PART EVACUATION

Where a HIGH alert state is declared in a controlled area (i.e. Backstage Area, hospitality area, etc.), the event may not be halted, so as not to cause panic. However, the stage manager will remain on stand-by to accept instruction and security/stewards will control access to that area.

FULL EVACUATION

Once the ELT have advised on a full evacuation, it will be carried out as per standing operating procedures in addition to the following instructions issued by the ELT as follows:

- Place all radio communication locations under police instruction.
- Advise site medical services.
- Direct any enquiries for casualty information to the police casualty bureau.
- Direct any press or media to the designated media centre or press officer.
- Arrange for electricians to supply emergency lighting (if required).
- Vendors that are not in the immediate danger will be instructed to remain with their units in position.
- No vehicle movement, other than emergency services, will be permitted once the site has been evacuated.
- Once the Arena is cleared all gates will be closed and staffed by security (L1s).
- All staff will be instructed to report to their R.V. Point (location to be advised at localised staff briefings) for accountability.
- Re-admission to the site will be decided by the senior police officer on site.
- Site security will maintain and preserve all evidence until the police are ready to take over.
- The emergency services R.V. Point and emergency access routes into the site are to be maintained at all times during the alert state.

Evacuation Operational Method

The evacuation of the Arena will be carried out in accordance with the arrangements contained in the local authority multi-agency contingency plan; the crowd will be managed by stewards under the direction of the ELT via Event Control.

Evacuation Alert Messages

The following coded messages will be used on all radio channels and the PA to step up or step down the alert state.

In the event of a situation or incident that could lead to a major incident or evacuation, the following message will be broadcast:

"WILL CONSTABLE ERIS PLEASE COME TO THE CONTROL ROOM"

This is a warning that the alert state has been raised to MEDIUM.

If the situation or incident is likely to result in a part or full evacuation of the site, the following message will be broadcast:

"WILL CONSTABLE ERIS COME TO THE CONTROL ROOM IMMEDIATELY"

This is a warning that the alert state has been upgraded to HIGH. All staff to stand by for further instructions on an evacuation of the site.

It may be that the incident is confined to a manageable area of the arena, if this is the case the following variation of the alert message will be broadcast:

"WILL CONSTABLE ERIS PLEASE COME TO... (I.e. Gate zero six)"

Emergency Evacuation Announcement

If a full evacuation is to be carried out the following announcement will be made over the main stage PA system:

"THIS IS AN EMERGENCY ANNOUNCEMENT. (DUE TO...) WE NEED TO EVACUATE THE ARENA IMMEDIATELY. STEWARDS AND POLICE WILL DIRECT YOU TO THE NEAREST AVAILABLE EXIT. PLEASE PROCEED QUIETLY AND CAREFULLY" (repeated).

If the evacuation is contained to a specific area of the arena, a local evacuation of the site will take place, under the control of the Police Silver Commander.

If the situation is contained the following message will be broadcast:

"THE MESSAGE FOR CONSTABLE ERIS IS CANCELLED"

Appendix A

Procedure for Transfer of Site Control to the Police

It is acknowledged that as a result of a serious incident in the category below or as indicated in the 'reason' section, control of the site must be transferred over to the police who have responsibility for co-ordinating the necessary combined emergency service response.

- A serious threat to public safety is evident.
- The potential for a serious public order problem exists.
- A serious crime has been committed.

RSES Ltd are therefore relinquishing command and control of the site and transferring responsibility to:

....Police.

Responsibility has been accepted by the signing of this document.

Name...

Rank..

Date...Time...

Reason..

....

....

....

Signature..

Appendix B

SECURITY/STEWARDS DUTY INSTRUCTIONS

- Make sure you read and understand these instructions carefully. If you have any doubts or questions then speak to your supervisor and ask for assistance.
- Remember audience safety is your responsibility! Ensure you have a copy of the Evacuation Procedures; read this continuously so that you are familiar with the messages that may be broadcast in an emergency.
- If you are working on an Exit Gate ensure that it is unlocked and the evacuation route leading to and from the gate is clear from OBSTRUCTIONS so that they are usable in an emergency. YOU must also have a radio for direct contact with Event Control.
- Be aware of and try to prevent any overcrowding or crushing. Report such incidents to your supervisor in addition to any safety hazards or site and building defects.
- Only allow persons entry to the arena if they have the correct ticket. Event pass holders must only be allowed access to areas that apply to the pass they are wearing. Always be on the look-out for forgeries!!
- Anyone considered unsuitable for immediate access to the venue must be referred to the licensed security staff in your location.
- Know the location of the nearest: SUPERVISOR, EXIT, FIRE FIGHTING EQUIPMENT, FIRST AID POST.
  Also know the nearest means of raising the fire alarm.
- Locate public service areas: i.e. Toilets, catering and merchandising, and familiarise yourself with the areas you are working in.
- Do not leave your position unattended at any time unless your life is in danger!
- Follow standard search procedures: male to male; female to female.
- Prohibited items are bottles, metal containers, cameras and recording equipment, alcohol and controlled drugs, folding chairs, fireworks, offensive weapons, or any item deemed to be a threat to public safety. Exceptions to the container rule may apply to the disabled, a pregnant woman and medically unfit persons.
  If in doubt, contact your supervisor for immediate assistance.

- Remember customer care. Be FRIENDLY, be POLITE be HELPFUL. Conduct your duties in a CALM and ORDERLY manner. Always observe the audience for persons in distress.
- You must wear your I.D. uniform at all times.

Appendix C

This checklist is designed to help deal with a telephoned bomb threat effectively and to record the necessary information.

Actions to be taken on receipt of a bomb threat:

- Switch on tape recorder (if connected)
- Tell the caller which town / district you are answering from
- Record the exact wording of the threat:

....

....

....

....

Ask the following questions:

- where is the bomb right now? ....

- when is it going to explode? ....

- what does it look like? ....

- what kind of bomb is it? ....

- what will cause it to explode? ....

- did you place the bomb? ....

- why? ....

- what is your name? ....

- what is your address? ....

- what is your telephone number? ....

Record time call completed: ....
Where automatic number reveal equipment is available, record number shown:

....

Inform the Senior Operations Manager -
Name and telephone number of the person informed:

....

Contact the police and the ELT. Time informed:..

Appendix C

The following part should be completed once the caller has hung up and the Senior Operations Manager has been informed.

Time and date of call:..

Length of call:...

Number at which call was received (i.e. your extension number):

ABOUT THE CALLER

Sex of caller: ....

Nationality:..

Age: ....

THREAT LANGUAGE (tick)
- ❏ Well spoken?
- ❏ Irrational?
- ❏ Taped message?
- ❏ Offensive?
- ❏ Incoherent?
- ❏ Message read by threat-maker?

CALLER'S VOICE (tick)
- ❏ Calm?
- ❏ Crying?
- ❏ Clearing throat?
- ❏ Angry?
- ❏ Nasal?
- ❏ Slurred?

- ❑ Excited?
- ❑ Stutter?
- ❑ Disguised?
- ❑ Slow?
- ❑ Lisp?
- ❑ Accent? If so, what type? _____
- ❑ Rapid?
- ❑ Deep?
- ❑ Hoarse?
- ❑ Laughter?
- ❑ Familiar? If so, whose voice did it sound like? _____

Appendix C

BACKGROUND SOUNDS (tick)

- ❑ Street noises?
- ❑ House noises?
- ❑ Animal noises?
- ❑ Crockery?
- ❑ Motor?
- ❑ Clear?
- ❑ Voice?
- ❑ Static?
- ❑ PA system?
- ❑ Booth?
- ❑ Music?
- ❑ Factory machinery?
- ❑ Office machinery?
- ❑ Other? (specify) ....

OTHER REMARKS

....

....

....

....

....

Signature ....

Date ....

Print name ....

5 THE SAFE MANAGEMENT OF ROCK CONCERTS UTILISING A BARRIER SAFETY SYSTEM (PRELIMINARY FINDINGS)

Introduction

This chapter firstly explores the global safety perspective in the live music industry and then goes on to explain the experiment carried out in the summers of 2004 and 2005 using the BLMS system pioneered by Patrick Jordan at MOJO barriers. The chapter is not aimed to be focused primarily on scientific or quantative developments but aims to describe the elements in layman's terms combining both quantative and qualitative evidence in a mixed paradigm exploration. It is clear from the narrative that there is room for four to five academic papers from this experiment and these will be published over the next two years. There is still a lot of work to be done in this area but it is clear that the live music industry can still do much to make the concert arena a safer place. The preoccupation with the bottom line is one key factor which militates against much of the concern voiced by those taking part in the project. However, if promoters wish to make concerts safer they would do well to at least consider the information contained in this chapter.

Crowd and Safety Management – a Global Perspective

In a global context the number of large- and super-scale music events taking place has tripled over the last decade. Not only has this increase in events caused a concomitant increase in the number of associated stewarding, crowd management and security companies participating in the industry, but it has also alerted these companies to the ever increasing threat of possible injury or death which accompany activities in all walks of life where mass crowds are gathered. Both crowd managers and promoters have also become aware of the associated risks of more sinister activities including terrorist attack and planned violence which has been recorded in isolated cases in Russia and Finland respectively. In all sectors of the industry, event managers, organisers and employees are more conscious of safety standards. This safety culture is not just the result of the knowledge gained during years of promoting and managing events but it is also related to the issues which effect the internal and external customers in relation to insurance and health developments in the music industry.

In tandem with an increase in safety standards governments worldwide have started to look at the way in which the licensing of events is carried out. In the UK for example, the Security Industry Authority (SIA) has started to enforce licensing on behalf of the government in a wide range of security related and crowd management areas. Although such a system of licensing activities within the security and crowd management industries brings with it the inevitable increase in staff training costs, the practice also enables the more professional development of the industry by chasing the 'cowboys' away.

Mark Harding, MD of Showsec International, states:

"Showsec was one of the founder crowd management companies which campaigned for the licensing of the security industry. Licensing and compulsory training brings value to an industry, the work it undertakes and the people who work within it. The greatest difficulty for crowd management companies is the continuing flow of emerging policies emanating from the legislation. This makes it exceptionally difficult to budget, resource and to agree contracts with our service partners. The SIA have a tremendous task ahead of them; we fully support their overall intentions."

Although such licensing initiatives are obviously good practice, the timescale within which activities have to be licensed is tight. Such a short timescale inevitably leads to a lack of available qualified licensed personnel to participate in the events planned for the next year.

The more events which take place the more likely a 'near miss' or serious accident is likely to occur and the security, stewarding, crowd safety and other related services are very conscious of the litigious nature of both internal and external clients. In line with this growing problem, promoters and crowd management companies are commissioning surveys, employing risk management consultants and research projects to reduce the possibility of such litigation.

One major issue linked to litigation which affects the industry globally is the increasing rise in insurance premiums. In a number of cases across Europe where Festivals and events have been found to be negligent an increased insurance premium has been levied on the previous years payment. This increase is caused by the spiralling costs of accidents and emergencies at events and the resultant associated costs of litigation. However, a more disturbing element of this is the increase in people deliberately injuring themselves to claim against festivals and concerts. The exacerbation of this trend has been fuelled by the rise internationally of ambulance chasers and companies specialising in suing the event industry over any accident or emergency. Even if a claim cannot be proved, the lower level claim of £3000 makes it not worth contesting by the promoter or event company, as the resultant legal costs are far less than those of a court appearance to contest a spurious claim. This Americanisation of the cultural industries (no offence to the Americans of course) has artificially driven up the costs of shows. In reality there are no more accidents and injuries today proportionately to what there were ten years ago. However people are more aware of the legal system across Europe and how they go about claiming against a company. As music industry lawyer Ben Challis states:

"Whist we don't quite have an ambulance chasing culture in most of Europe I think the development of such a culture is imminent. Personal injury claims are rising and lawyers (being lawyers) can see a huge growth area for fees. Certainly the availability of lawyers on a 'no win, no fee' basis has meant many more claims and settlements and of course the direct result of this is a rise in the cost of insurance for promoters, artists and venues."

In a world of increasing tension the concert environment like all other mass gatherings is not only affected by rising costs and litigation but also in a small

Front of stage corner barrier at Roskilde.

number of recent cases to planned violence (North Karelia in Finland) and terrorism (Kiev in Russia and the Atlanta Olympic Games). It was inevitable that gatherings of 30,00 plus would eventually become a target for those wishing to make political statements. The advent of new technology in the search of people and places and new security developments has made planned mass gatherings much easier to manage and monitor. This is especially relevant with the Olympic Games taking place in London in 2012. All of those planning mass crowd events are aware of the changing environment and have created supporting contingencies and emergency plans to support such eventualities which are of course few and far between. Planned violence at a very small number of events in Finland and Holland has caused crowd managers to think again about their planning processes and it is clear that as festival attendances rise that promoters and event managers are doing everything to make the total experience for the attendee a paramount feature of their festivals and events. Unfortunately the concert is a prime target for anti social and over social activity as it is a place where a mass crowd congregates for up to seven days, making it a possible for all kinds of activities to take place. The difficulty of preparing for such activity is highlighted by Gerard van Duykeren of ICMS in Holland who states:

"As a crowd management company we do not have the resources and authority to have access to intelligence and information that is available to Governments. Therefore, we cannot act at the early stages of a terrorist threat. What we can do is give extra attention to the perimeter observation (CCTV) and mobile teams with security staff members who patrol around all access and entrances to the event. During the event we can make sure that our staff are alert and carefully trained to be proactive and vigilant in such situations. We also need to be prepared for the aftermath of an attack ensuring that the operation, systems and contingencies are at the highest level i.e. to deal with evacuation and damage limitation."

Research is being carried out into a wide range of areas including barrier pressure and barrier systems, fill capacities at the front of stage, ingress and egress, crowd behaviour and crowd psychology. All of these elements build towards the development of a safer concert environment and enable the promoter and other concert providers to plan effectively and efficiently for problems in the arena at the festival or other concert event. The ILMC, in conjunction with Buckinghamshire Chilterns University College and OSHA, created a Risk Assessment Tool to be used Europe-wide to ensure that all event workers, whatever the size of the event, had access to a tool to enable them to work more effectively at events. The risk assessment is only one factor in a web of developments linked to the event, but more important is the risk analysis and management. Anyone can create a risk assessment but how many people analyse or manage risk correctly utilising a fluid risk analysis reviewed throughout the concert process?

In the summers of 2005 and 2006 the Centre for Crowd Management Studies at BCUC in conjunction with the ILMC Safety Focus Group, Patrick Jordan of MOJO barriers, Henrik Bondo Nielsen from Roskilde Festival and Gerard Von Durkynen of ICMS carried out research into single and triple barrier systems. This project was linked to pressure and heart rate using the MOJO pressure system, video and photographic evidence, heart rate monitors and audience questionnaires. The outcome of the research identifies that barrier systems at a mass crowd event when not managed as part of the event process are particulary dangerous and that severe measures have to be put into place to ensure that the crowd is coached and managed properly throughout the event. Some promoters and event managers prefer multi-barrier to single barrier systems. Jim Fiddler from Australian Event Production backs the research up by stating:

"The single barrier system is a nightmare. It gives us as crowd managers

High density crowd, front of stage.

the inability to limit the number of patrons in front of stage; it also has severe limitations on any rescue initiative during front of stage collapse. Such barriers also do not enable the rotation of the crowd in front of the barrier which causes undue strain and stress on individuals. Promoters and event organisers need to invest in triple barrier systems to ensure the safety of the audience."

However, the single barrier system has been used successfully by an enormous number of promoters. Through their crowd management teams creating management and stewarding structures to suit the crowd and the genre of music few accidents have taken place. One key aspect driving the discussion on barrier systems is the weighing up of the tensions relating to the management of the barrier and the reasons for the attendee to visit an event. The creation of systems or frameworks, which reduce the enjoyment of the audience whilst showing no benefit to the safety of the public or those working at an event, may turn attendees away from such events.

It is clear from the research that if such barriers are not managed carefully (as in any barrier system) then there are issues in regard to the safety of such a system.

The study also calls into question the present use of the golden circle, revealing it as a mode which can cause increased pressure rather than alleviating it. In the case of recent research into the Golden Circle activity it is clear that such a system will only work if its purpose, organisation and pricing structure are clearly communicated to the audience well in advance of the show.

Another major concern for crowd managers and security companies is associated with the 'cultural behaviour' of fans. The control of the 2-4% of the fans in the audience who practise moshing, crowd surfing, skanking and stage diving is becoming more difficult. Roskilde Festival has effectively all but eradicated this behaviour through careful planning and organisation. The Roskilde model is worth focusing upon as it identifies major elements which could be reproduced to great effect in any concert environment. At an early stage the Roskilde Festival website introduces the audience to the type of behaviour expected at the festival. This 'coaching' grew out of the disaster which took place in 2000 where nine audience members lost their lives. Roskilde reiterates that it does not tolerate what is termed as 'anti social' behaviour. The audience is also coached during the event to behave in a way which will allow all of the fans to enjoy themselves.

Alongside this audience 'coaching' Roskilde employs three levels of crowd management: the spotter, employed specifically to identify people in the crowd who are in trouble or causing trouble, the steward who is employed to deal with these cases when spotted, and the manager who manages the stewards. The pit set up at Roskilde is ingenious. Two front pits housing 580 people form the primary barrier, two pits housing 850 people house the secondary barrier and the tertiary barrier hold the rest of the mass crowd. To take up a place in any of the four pits the audience has to queue to gain access. At the end of each act the pits are cleared and a new audience allowed in for the next artist. By facilitating this procedure no member of the audience is subject to a high level of pressure for

Artiste's performance causing 180° turn of audience.

more than one act. The maximum pressure in the front pit at Roskilde is 4.30kN, extremely high for a crowd of 580 people. The maximum crowd pressure at the Leeds Festival on the single barrier was 6.30kN, however this was from an audience of 55,000 people. If the pressures at Roskilde and Leeds were taken proportionately then the pressure at Roskilde is far greater per individual than that at Leeds. The pressure from the mass audience behind the tertiary barrier at Roskilde however is only 1.85kN which indicates that by removing the most vociferous and rowdy audience members form the mass crowd and controlling them carefully, the pressure can be reduced in the rest of the crowd.

At both Leeds and Reading Festivals, which employed a single barrier at this time, it was clear that a management strategy adequate to support this level of pressure was in place. However, it is clear that such a strategy does put the pit team under heavy pressure during the event. It is also clear from the research that cultural differences and staff expectations have to be tempered with audience expectations of the event.

The development of new technology including clean internal PA systems, scoreboards and big screens has made the development of crowd education and emergency and other messaging easier. By being able to contact the crowd at any time the organiser and crowd manager are able to get a message quickly, effectively and efficiently to the crowd. Constant reminders about exits and behaviour enable a crowd to be controlled more easily. One further key to establishing a rapport with the audience and to understand what to expect at present and future events is to undertake psychological and social profiling which enables the concert organiser to understand more about the audience who will attend a specific event. Know your audience. At a number of festivals recently, unsavoury elements have crept into the audience and fighting and brawling has caused immense problems not only for the organisers but for other members of the audience. Questionnaire profiling and quick dissemination of results can establish problems within the crowd. Whereas mass crowd behaviour can be identified through a number of means, the reduction of problems with individuals can be put down to the type of welfare operation

Crowd pressure clearly showing on attendee's chest at front of stage.

at the event. Penny Mellor, a well-known welfare consultant in the music industry states:

> "Welfare provision identifies an accessible place where anyone with difficulties can get their problems sorted on an individual basis. This in itself can reduce and prevent potential crowd problems. We have learned more over the last 20 years in the identification of problems and how to deal with them effectively and efficiently and this knowledge makes people less disgruntled if they perceive that the organisers care about them."

Linked to welfare and mass crowd control is the element of command and control. In many countries across the globe this vital area is carried out either in a piecemeal fashion where in some cases each body (Crowd Management Team, ELT, Police, Environmental Health, etc.) have their own hut with their own communication system, or in isolation. This in reality is ineffective and inefficient as if anything goes wrong on the day or there is a problem at the event each service deals with the problem in their own way instead of creating a collective and cohesive approach. At the Olympic Stadium (Telstra) in Australia a specialist room is housed where everyone involved with the event is housed for the duration. This includes staff members from bus and rail companies, the ambulance services, site managers and anyone else with a vested interest in the system. If a problem occurs, coordinated response can take place. The creation of command and control procedures must take place to enable a swift and efficient response.

Although these events are all topical, one of the most important developments of the past decade is the institution of CCTV cameras into the event. These cameras have two major functions: firstly to identify if members of the audience who are in trouble and thus enabling a swift and efficient response to those in trouble and the second function is that of deterrent. The placing of cameras in areas of perceived tension and areas where problems may occur makes those with criminal tendencies and also those who tend to have high spirits continually throughout the concert to think twice about committing an act which may spark trouble of cause discomfort to others. Although the effectiveness of CCTV at concerts has not been researched in detail, the results of research in football point to a decrease of over 65% in incidents at points of tension in football grounds. Such research cannot be ignored, especially considering the rise in violent behaviour at some events and the spectre of the terrorist.

To conclude, it is clear that the industry is well aware of the work at present needed to ensure that events and concerts across the world are safe for those attending and that no matter how much money it costs, to make these safe some investment must be made to ensure the safety of the customer. New laws to prevent ambulance chasing like those introduced in Australia would be a start. Some form of European policy on levels of experience needed to put on or staff an event would also be welcome. However, more important than all of these is the willingness of all of those involved in the command and control of an event to work together towards a safe and healthy event environment. To help to develop a safer concert environment, the Centre for Crowd Management Research with the help of the International Live Music Conference Safety Focus Group, the Roskilde Festival, ICMS and the Nijmegen Festival conducted both primary and secondary research to establish whether what was thought to be causing deaths, near misses and injuries at live concerts was actually the prime cause of such events.

The Purpose of the Research

The purpose of this pilot study was to examine and ratify the social and scientific factors underpinning opinion and conjecture in relation to the pressure exerted by crowds on primary, secondary and tertiary barriers at concert events. The final research for this project was carried out in 2006 at ten events across Europe. This pilot study was also carried out at a selection of outdoor concerts and festivals across Europe but on a smaller scale than the final research.

During the past five decades, hundreds of people have lost their lives and thousands have been injured in crowd related incidents at various events across the world. The purpose of this study is to present social and scientific evidence to support the belief that there are ways to stop, or reduce the impact of such catastrophes. The study focuses on three major concert events: the Leeds Festival in the UK in 2004, the Roskilde Festival in Denmark in 2005, and the Nijmegen Festival in Holland in 2005. The utilisation of results from Roskilde Festival is especially pertinent as nine people lost their lives at this event in 2000. The sample consisted of audiences of between 55,000 and 75,000 people and questionnaire samples of 2000 concert attendees in Nijmegen and Roskilde were taken to underpin the research carried out. A hybrid methodology was utilised to enable a comparison of social and scientific data. Supporting literature underpins the conclusions of the study which back up opinion and conjecture that a small proportion of the audience are responsible for a large proportion of the pressure at concerts, and that careful management of the audience can reduce the danger caused by the build-up and maintenance of pressure at the barrier.

Introduction to the Research

In a 1992 seminar paper, American planner John Fruin highlighted that virtually all crowd related incident deaths were caused by *'compressive asphyxia'* and not as previously assumed by commentators as a result of being trampled by a panicked crowd. As there is no fixed point at which death occurs from being subjected to an intolerable pressure load it is difficult to identify the major causes of such pressure without a combination of social and scientific research. A British Home Office (1973) report cited two fatal cases:

a) Death of one male was estimated to have taken place when subjected to an estimated load of 1400 lbs (over 6kN) for 15 seconds.

b) A man died when subjected to an estimated load of 260 lbs (1.1kN.) for 4.5 minutes.

From these two cases it can be estimated that both high pressure for a short duration and medium pressure for a sustained period can both lead to death by asphyxiation. A series of experiments undertaken by Hopkins, Pountney, Heyes and Sheppard (1993) concluded that males and females were able to withstand pressure loads in the region of 140 - 180 lbs. (approximately 0.8kN) when they were able to push against a fixed barrier to gain breathing space. Current medical opinion is that in conditions where the human body is subjected to a higher static pressure load of approximately 300lbs (1.1kN) on the chest cavity beyond 2½ - 3 minutes the brain begins to starve of oxygen and permanent injury may be caused. Beyond 3 minutes death may occur at any time.

Thus the demographics of an audience have a bearing on the sustainability of life during increased or sustained pressure loading from mass crowd activity. The sex, age, endurance, shape (morphic development), cultural activity and indeed culture itself also have a bearing on the pressure loading as differing cultures, dietetic and muscular development can signify the susceptibility or resistance to the onset of pressure in any given context. For example the average weight of an American citizen and thus size, compared to the same dimensions of a Chinese citizen, indicates that more Chinese citizens would be able to fit into a square metre space at a concert than American citizens and this would have an immediate effect on crowd density. (If the concert were purely American or Chinese audience-based – *Still 1997*.) In such cases the density is decreased, even though the pressure may be the same when measuring the two audience groups.

This demographic effect is highlighted in research by Upton in 1996 and 2004 which identifies that an intolerable pressure load can be caused in two related but mutually exclusive events at a concert, firstly by high crowd density or a lateral or dynamic surge that converts to a static load. In such circumstances it is common for the audience in front of a barrier to create a backward force by pushing away from the barrier in order to gain a space within which to breathe. Such a movement may subject people 3-4 metres away from the barrier to a two-way horizontal load as the audience at the back press forward and the audience at the front press backward. Secondly, a crowd collapse may occur as a result of a dynamic or lateral surge which may lead to individuals fainting or falling due to the ground conditions at the event, or the practice of anti-social cultural behaviour by the audience. This behaviour is related directly to the demographic profile of the audience and is dependent on the genre of music at the event. If a crowd collapse occurs an intolerable vertical load may be imposed on the audience members at the bottom of a pile of bodies in a very quick time-frame. A crowd collapse can occur *anywhere* within a crowd mass and not just at a barrier.

Although this paper does not focus upon cultural behaviour within the audience, to gain a better understanding of the results and conclusions, a section on the cultural behaviour experienced at the concert events researched is included. Cultural behaviour at rock concerts can be a major cause for concern. *Moshing* is an American term used to describe what seventies Punk Rock culture called *slam dancing*. Moshing is a dance ritual during which people slam into each other. Although it appears to be a violent action it is not intended to be. It can nevertheless result in the participants receiving cuts, bruises or more serious injuries such as broken bones. The act of moshing generally takes place in the '*mosh pit*'. This term is used to describe the general area that moshing takes place and should not be confused with the area in front of stage known as the *primary pit*. A mosh pit can start spontaneously anywhere in the crowd and should therefore be regarded more as an activity and not an actual place.

The term moshing is also often used in broader terms to refer to a number of other activities. *Crowd Surfing* is one of these activities. It involves crowd members lifting an individual above the crowd so that the person can roll or swim over the heads of the crowd. Normally a surfer will move toward the stage with the intention to continue involvement in this type of cultural activity. People have been known to bring surfboards into a show for the purposes of crowd surfing. There have been numerous injuries recorded as a result of such activity. These injuries have included neck and/or head injuries to people that have been kicked, or spinal injuries caused as a result of the crowd surfer falling, or being dropped onto the ground. The added danger brought about by such an action is when a fallen surfer causes other audience members to fall, creating an intolerable pressure load. There have been serious injuries reported as a result of crowd surfing. For example, Sara Jean Green wrote in the *Seattle Times* (2002) that the parents of 14-year-old Scott Stone reached an out-of-court settlement for permanent brain damage which it was alleged was the result of a crowd surfing incident in 1996. Green claimed that there had been 1,000 reported injuries from just 15 American concerts in 2001. In America there have also been allegations of sexual assault and even rape of female surfers who have been dragged down and stripped of their clothing by males in the crowd.

Stage Diving is exactly what the term implies. It is the act of a performer or member of the audience diving from the stage into the crowd. The intention is then that the crowd will support that person above their heads while they crowd surf. Unfortunately the activity is not risk free. In 1994 a young man died at a club in New York as the result of what appears to be a stage diving incident. It was alleged that a security man pushed the victim off the stage; the security denied the allegation and alleged that the victim was stage diving (Rogers 1996). However in contemporary festivals and events the practice of stage diving has been all but eradicated by the introduction of pit security and the development of higher stages.

Pogoing is a seventies punk rock dance ritual, during which the crowd jumps up and down in unison, often giving gladiatorial salutes. The activity is still popular with a range of rock culture crowds. While this activity appears to be harmless pogoing can present a problem at green-field sites, particularly where there is a steep gradient downwards toward the stage. After prolonged or heavy rain the field becomes very slippery and a mass of people all jumping up and down in unison can easily cause a dynamic surge similar to a landslide which might result in a crowd collapse. With the return of the third wave of punk or nu punk this phenomenon has recently resurfaced in mainstream rather than minority interest music.

Skanking is another peculiar term. It was originally used as a term for slam dancing or as a prelude to crowd surfing. The term is now more likely to be used to describe a mosh pit activity where a circle forms within a crowd. In extreme cases the circle can act like a whirlpool. The size and duration of this rotating circle is dependent on the number of people drawn into it. Skanking has been known to cause a crowd collapse which, as has been previously stated, can lead to intolerable pressure loads being imposed on those unfortunate enough to be at the bottom of a pile of bodies. Research into this phenomenon identifies its practice as one of the major elements responsible for increased pressure in the pit.

To combat and contain various aspects of this cultural activity, the creation of crowd barrier systems began in the 1960s after a number of problems relating to stage invasions and cancelled shows. The initial barriers were indoors where venue orchestra pits were adapted to enable the crowd managers at the time to control the crowd effectively. However, over time it became more important to ensure that the crowd was not only controlled but safe in the concert environment. Thus, a number of barrier companies developed barriers to assist in the safe development of crowd activity. The system utilized in this study is the MOJO Barrier system. The MOJO Barrier System has been developed over the past decade to test and ensure the safety of the crowd by constantly monitoring and improving the system to make sure that a contemporary approach to the way in which the barrier is utilised affords safe practices at events all over the world. Each of the three events scrutinised for this study all utilised a MOJO barrier system.

The three events comprise the Leeds, Roskilde and Fields of Rock (Nijmegen) festivals. The Leeds Festival Barrier was a single length of barrier housing a mass crowd of 55,000. The barrier fronted a single stage. The festival attracted a specific punk, grunge, indie and rock audience and bands including Green Day, The Lost Prophets and the Dropkick Murphys were on the bill. The Nijmegen Festival Barrier was a three barrier system with a large pit adjacent to a double stage (housing 3000) and a smaller secondary pit behind the primary pit (housing 1000). The third barrier separated the mass audience from those in the front two pits. This festival attracted an older audience than either of the other two festivals studied and the artist bill reflected this comprising a mix of older rock and thrash artists (Black Sabbath and Slayer) and new bands comprising members of older rock bands in new formats. The Roskilde Festival Barrier comprises two front pits adjacent to the stage housing 580 attendees with two secondary pits adjacent to the two front pits each holding

850 attendees. The mass crowd is housed behind a third barrier. The mix of music at the Roskilde Festival is more eclectic than the other two festivals and on the day of the experiment Jimmy Eat World, The Foo Fighters, Green Day and Duran Duran were the bands on the Orange Stage, a single stage construction. Of course the demographics of the attendees have also to be taken into consideration as by far the largest age range of attendees at Leeds is under 18 and that of Roskilde 19-21. Age, sex, number of festivals attended and genre are all important factors in the way that a crowd behave and how they are subsequently managed.

Owing to the complex nature of this study a single paradigm could not be utilised and therefore a hybrid methodology was employed.

The Type of Methods Used in the Research

The development of a study utilising both quantitative and qualitative research methods supports the theory that a hybridisation of methodologies should be utilised where this practice best suits the purpose of the research. In the case of this study where both scientific (pressure barrier readings, demographic data collection) and social science (participant observation, visual representation) elements are key to the research the utilisation of such a methodology has an underpinning rationale.

The methods employed for this study were as follows:

Pressure Loading: The MBX system developed by MOJO Barriers was utilised to measure the pressure at distinct points in the barrier system at the three concerts. The system measures the downward pressure on specific points in the barrier every five seconds and sends the readings to a monitor under the stage. The monitor is time-coded to ensure that the other systems employed can be compared at any instant with data from other sources which is time-coded in the same way.

Video and CCTV: The concert audience was videoed throughout the time that the crowd was being monitored. The cameras were focused on specific points to enable correlation with the pressure at the barrier at any given time. Thus using time coding instantaneous pressure and video readings could be viewed.

Heart Rate Monitoring: Ten volunteers were fitted with heart rate monitors during the concert using the Polar Heart Rate Monitoring System. The results were time-coded and downloaded after the event and graphically represented so that changes in heart rate could be compared with other elements of the test.

Stage and Crowd Observation: An open line from the camera to the time code system was recorded. A subject gave a running commentary of what was happening on stage to ensure that if a high pressure reading was recorded this information could be fed back to the group.

Photographic Evidence: Over six hundred photographs were taken of the crowd and the barrier to illustrate the pressure readings on the barrier. This evidence is used to back up participant observation.

Audience Observation: Each member of the group made notes from participant observation on any action or reaction which occurred during the festival. This could then be compared with video evidence.

Questionnaires: Questionnaires were distributed to 1000 audience members in the pit at both the Nijmegen and Roskilde shows to gain information relating to the study.

Analysis: Visual and mathematical analyses were key factors in identifying the characteristics and development of the study results and conclusions.

The Results from the Research

The results of this study indicate that effective management of a barrier system reduces the main pressure in the festival auditorium and is thus a more effective and efficient tool in the reduction of fatalities and injury than a non-managed barrier system. Secondly, from further analysis the utilisation of a two barrier system where a golden circle is utilised is not an efficient reducing factor in crowd pressure at events where information is not imparted to audience exactly.

At the Leeds Festival the maximum pressure exerted on the primary barrier was recorded at 6.40kNm, whereas the maximum pressure recorded at the primary barrier at Roskilde was 3.40kNm. The Maximum pressure recorded at the primary barrier during the Nijmegen Festival was 2.85kNm. The artists playing at the time when such pressure was exerted were The Lost Prophets (Leeds), Green Day (Roskilde) and Slayer (Nijmegen). The lowest maximum pressures recorded during crowd activity at the three festivals respectively were 0.5kNm, 0.75kNm, 0.3kNm. The first factor which became apparent during the analysis of the results was that a direct relationship could be identified between the pressure recorded at the barrier and the tempo of the music. In general the higher the tempo of the music the more pressure was exerted on the barrier. This is supported by research by Kemp (2004) into the tempos of punk and nu punk artists, where crowd activity is heightened by an increase in tempo. In the case of Green Day and Slayer the tempo of both artists reached 210bpm on occasion. The average tempo of many Black Sabbath Songs is in the region of 80-100bpm. The difference between the high tempo artists and those with lower tempo songs can be identified from the pressure readings taken during the three festivals. This can be seen most clearly at the Nijmegen festival where the maximum pressure exerted on the front barrier for Black Sabbath was 1.85kNm whilst the maximum pressure exerted for Slayer was 2.85kNm. This is replicated at each of the three festivals identifying the tempo of music as a contributory factor to the pressure exerted on the primary barrier.

Video, photographic and pressure sensor evidence indicates that the two activities related most closely to increased pressure at the barrier are those of skanking and mass crowd activity. The combination of these two activities may cause an outward acceleration forcing audience members to push other attendees causing a ripple effect which not only increases pressure but pushes the crowd outward inducing instability and the possibility of collapse. In extreme cases this can cause a domino effect where a large area of crowd collapses in a curved motion following the contours of the barrier. The mosh and skanking phenomena was studied in detail at Nijmegen and it is clear that only a few or even one person can start the movement with a push and this then quickly spreads in a lateral manner. Once the spread starts, the mosh can go out of control. The main mosh lasts only minutes as it then recedes into a smaller pit and then at the end of the song disappears. It is clear from video evidence that a mosh only starts when the musical tempo is sufficiently fast to enable a timed move forward or backward, if the tempo decreases the mosh invariably tends to stop. This is however not the case in mass moshing where the activity can last up to four songs. However the majority of moshers become tired and do other things whilst the hardcore fan tries to start the activity up again.

It is also clear however that cultural differences, demographics, musical genre, artist behaviour, location of the site and topography also play a vital role in the pressure exerted on a barrier by a crowd; however, this experiment goes some way in the support of a well managed three barrier system in the development of a safe concert environment.

A comparison of pressure at the Roskilde and Leeds festivals highlights large pressure differences at the two primary barriers. The maximum pressure on the Leeds barrier is 6.40kNm compared with a maximum pressure of 3.40kNm at Roskilde. However the Leeds festival maximum is recorded from a mass crowd of 55,000 spread over a distance of approximately 110 metres. The maximum crowd pressure at Roskilde is recorded for a crowd of 580 over a distance of 11.12 metres. If the Roskilde pressure were projected over the same distance as the Leeds crowd pressure the pressure would be recorded at 33.62kNm. The crowd mass examined at Leeds is 94.8 times larger than that examined at Roskilde to ascertain the maximum pressure reading. If the Leeds crowd mass was projected onto that of Roskilde the maximum projected pressure would be 322.41kNm. Such readings of course would not transfer owing to the many extraneous factors.

It is clear however, that by a self-selection process, those within the mass crowd at Roskilde who focus on a wide range of cultural (front of stage) activities gravitate towards the front pit at the festival. Whereas at Leeds these audience members were mixed in with the mass crowd, at both Roskilde and Nijmegen the self-reflection into a smaller managed pit system isolated to some extent those causing major pressure surges and also increased their manageability in the context of the whole event. However, what this also indicates is that a large pressure loading can be caused by a small number of people and thus points to management capabilities between small and large audiences. It is also possible that because at both Nijmegen and Roskilde the audiences are far away from the stage the incentive to take part in any cultural behaviour may be lessened.

However, from observations at other events it is clear that skanking and moshing are not confined to the front of stage area but can take place anywhere in the auditorium and as such periodic or sustained pressure is dependent on the genre of music, the cultural behaviour and other aspects such as climate.

There are a number of significant factors which can be identified from the pressure readings at Roskilde which directly relate to the pressure exerted at the primary barrier and indicate why there is such a reduction in pressure at the secondary and tertiary barriers. At Leeds the mass crowd of 55,000 exert a pressure of 6.40kNm on the primary barrier. However, at Roskilde a mass crowd of similar proportion exert a maximum pressure of 2.30kNm on the tertiary barrier. At the Nijmegen Festival a similar sized mass crowd exerts a maximum pressure of 1.65kNm at the tertiary barrier. The results indicate a reduced mass crowd pressure at both Roskilde and Nijmegen in comparison with the Leeds maximum crowd pressure. One caveat of course must be applied here and that relates to the mean crowd pressures at both Leeds and Roskilde. These mean pressures are fairly equal showing that the overall crowd pressure discounting the peaks is fairly similar across the two festivals. The combined pressure at the three barriers at Roskilde is 6.60kNm, 0.2kNm more than the maximum pressure exerted on the single barrier at Leeds. However, the disaggregated pressure on all of the barriers at Roskilde at its maximum primary barrier pressure is over 3.0kNm less than at the Leeds Festival. At Nijmegen, where there were two stages, the overall maximum pressure is approximately equal at both stages with a maximum pressure of 0.25kNm in the centre of the two stages (between stage A and stage B). At Roskilde the maximum aggregated pressure at stage left is 6.60kNm, almost double the maximum pressure at stage right which reaches 3.85kNm. Although at the two barrier stage in Nijmegen the maximum pressure exerted is 0.25kNm, this is not the case with the pen system at Roskilde where the maximum pressure is recorded close to the centre of the stage. Video and photographic evidence show that the maximum pressure is not exerted at a 90° angle to the primary barrier but at a 45° angle to the barrier with the audience facing the centre of the stage rather than forward. This is peculiar to a pen system with a runway from the mixing tower to the stage as the natural movement for the crowd is towards centre stage. In a single stage show without the runway the audience tend to face at between 75° and 90° to the stage. The reason for this directional force is the focusing of the audience on the centre of the stage where both the lead singer and drummer of most bands reside.

At Leeds Festival the set-up is such that once the audience is let into the auditorium they make their way en masse towards the stage. Positioning of the audience is indiscriminate and thus members of the mass audience may elect to stay at the front of the barrier for the whole festival. At Roskilde the mass audience congregates behind the tertiary barrier but audience members can elect to queue for the front four pens, two primary stage right and left and two secondary, stage right and left. The queuing audience is then let into the primary and secondary pens. At the end of each act the pens are cleared and queuing has already begun for the next act this is the norm at most festivals in Europe and is a major reason why attendees opt to go to such festivals as there is freedom of choice where they situate themselves for the whole festival.

With such a system the most die-hard and active fans of each band have the opportunity to opt to be in the primary and secondary pits. This act separates these attendees from the mass audience. As these primary and secondary pens are easily accessible the monitoring and management of these attendees is easily managed. The use of spotters to identify problems, stewards to deal with the problems and managers to manage the problems mean that Roskilde has an efficient and effective system in place to reduce the pressure in the mass crowd.

The barrier system at Nijmegen, where a large primary and a smaller secondary pit were in use, also reduced the mass crowd pressure on the front and secondary barriers. However the usage of a double stage system did cause some problems with lateral pressure movement and some incidents of small crowd collapse when the main band took the stage. However, the pressure dissipation helped with the reduction of pressure at pinch points. The reversal of the two barrier capacities may have been more manageable as the main audience would have been placed in a smaller area making their management easier.

At Leeds the management system is focused on the periphery of the audience. This is to ensure that the front of stage pit, the stage left and stage right audience and those at the back of the crowd mass are supported by the stewards and crowd managers. The only issue with such a large crowd at a single barrier which is also an issue at the tertiary barrier at both Roksilde and Nijmegen is that of reaching anyone in trouble at the centre of the audience. Thus contingencies are arranged to enable this.

It can be ascertained from the research that the artist also plays a vital role in the way an audience react and thus the pressure exerted on the barrier. At Nijmegen artist (A) brought an alien object into the audience causing the possibility of problems with suffocation, over excitement and crowd collapse during this interlude. At Roskilde artist (B) ran from the stage up the walkway and onto the lighting tower to play guitar. The sudden reaction of the crowd in the front two pen sets was to turn 180° to watch the artist on the front of the tower. This not only exerted severe pressure on the back of the barrier system through the reversing of the audience but it also caused high pressure on the tertiary barrier as audience members pushed forward to try and catch a glimpse of the artist. Conversely artist (C) at Roskilde in a two-hour show played less than 50 minutes music, playing the crowd and making sure that when the audience was at a height or frenzy that they were calmed accordingly. Here the artist is taking responsibility in some way for the behaviour of the crowd.

Linked directly to the focus on crowd pressure is the development of the 'Golden Circle' at major concert events. The two functions of the Golden Circle are first and foremost to generate extra income by charging a premium to those in the 'Golden Circle' and secondly almost perceived by default to alleviate pressure at the front of the primary barrier in the auditorium and secondly. However it is clear from the aforementioned research that the Golden Circle does not alleviate the crowd pressure as it is selective in the way in which attendees are able to gain access to the circle itself. The most vociferous and die-hard fans are not usually the people who find out about or are able to access the 'Golden Circle'. From research carried out in Hyde Park at the Red Hot Chilli Peppers concert it is clear that the main body of the artist following is sited at the secondary barrier and not the primary barrier and this was borne out by the increased pressure at this barrier and the number of attendees that had to be extracted from the audience. These results however are skewed by the uneven distribution of attendees caused by a foreign body at the entrance to the auditorium which forced two-thirds of the concert audience towards stage right rather than stage left increasing the pressure on one side of the barrier. Thus at this event the Golden Circle did not serve the purpose of reducing the crowd pressure but caused dissent in the audience as mainstream fans perceive that they had not been informed of the Golden Circle and were expecting to be at the front of the auditorium. It must be pointed out here that at the time of this concert the Golden Circle was a relatively new addition to rock and indie events and as such the audience were not aware of the structure of this entity. Today, however, this would not be the case as the Golden Circle idea is now well established in the concert psyche and expected to be closer to the stage. If the Golden Circle were filled by a queuing system for each artist and then emptied at the end of each act it should follow that the most vociferous and die-hard fans would gain a place in the circle and thus the pressure would be alleviated in this way. At Eminem at Milton Keynes Bowl a wristband system was employed to enable die-hard fans of the artist to enter a pit nearer to the front of the auditorium. A primary pit contained the band's friends, small children and women. In this way you reduce the pressure on those less able to stand the pressure and also allow the most vociferous and die-hard fans places closer to the event. This should reduce the pressure in this case, although more research would need to be done to ascertain whether this was the case.

The Conclusions Gained from the Research

The pilot crowd pressure barrier study was an attempt to explore a combination of social behaviour and scientific evidence in the context of pressure at concerts. The results of the study indicate the following conclusions:

A well managed and monitored three barrier system reduces the crowd pressure at the primary, secondary and tertiary barriers significantly. It can be seen that at any large concert where a single barrier system is utilised that there are a number of phenomena associated with the mass audience that make the use of a single barrier system difficult to manage. The first is the mass wave which starts at the centre or back of the crowd and gathers momentum forward. The most recent example of this phenomena was at the Oasis Concert in the summer of 2005 where a large wave swept forward at the City of Manchester Stadium. Such phenomena are terrfying not only for the audience but for those who are managing the crowd. The mass crowd wave causes crowd collapse, individual slippage and a pressure on the barrier which can cause either forward barrier movement or total barrier collapse. The origin of such waves is unclear but from the study of video evoidence it is clear that the origin is not caused by a large body of the audience but a small proportion of those in the auditorium causing a forward movement. The momentum of such a wave is frightening as it builds steadily until the wave moves both laterally and medially as it disspates from the primary barrier. At Nijmegen a similar small wave was caused in the primary pit which caused a domino crowd collapse. However, owing to the fact that the crowd in the pit was relatively small, staff and other audience members were able to pull those that had fallen up from the floor.

The utilisation of a pressure barrier system at a concert, alerts managers early on to any possible points of tension within the crowd in the arena. If this is utilised on a double or triple basis then this can be said for any given time and at any given barrier. If the pressure barrier system is coupled with CCTV or video surveillance of the audience then the promoter or crowd manager has two ways of ensuring that they are apprised early of any problems occurring in the crowd. Rather than developing large mass crowd pens at an event it is clear from the aforementioned research that the use of small pens to contain the more vociferous fans allows access for stewards, managers and spotters if problems occur. It is common sense that the more access that the crowd manager has to the audience the safer the audience will be as the crowd manager and their staff are able to spot early and control the way in which the audience are controlled. By using spotters and simple queuing mechanisms the crowd manager can increase the effective and efficient reduction of points of tension within the crowd. Identifying the audience type and ensuring that the fans associated with the genre are carefully profiled a comfort zone is created within which both the audience member and the staff exist. This helps to ensure a safe working and concert going environment. By removing the hard core fan from the mass crowd and managing these fans in an active way the safety of the mass crowd becomes less of an issue. The creation of a one barrier, one pit scenario does not enable fans of a particular artist to access the best possible position to view that artist from. Conversely, the splitting of the audience increases the management responsibilities of the crowd manager. Instead of focusing effort on one area and thus enabling a single operation the management focus is on three areas which increases the focus of the management team and subdivides the possibility of opportunity. In the case of a three or four band bill with carefully chosen artists the queuing procedure or policy can vastly reduce the time that audience members spend at the front of the barrier. This is more problematic where only one artist is playing and from experience of many large events it is clear that large gaps between artists and poorly billed shows can lead to issues with fans in the auditorium. To utilise a triple barrier system works wonders at a festival, but it is more difficult to administer at a one day event. However with careful planning and the correct line-up this is not difficult to develop.

From two recent pieces of research it is also clear that the control of the crowd by the artist significantly reduces discomfort and injury at a concert and conversely the artist can whip a crowd up into a frenzy causing severe crowd problems if they wish. Recent research by Claire Mcleod (2005) identified that artists were often so wrapped up in their performance that they were unable to recognise what state an audience were in during a performance. It was also clear from this research that many artists actively geared their shows to reducing the way in which the audience showed their appreciation for the artist. However it is also clear that in certain types of music, namely thrash metal and punk (Kemp 2005), that the artists actively encouraged aggressive and anti-social behaviour. It is clear however on talking to such artists that they are becoming aware of the role that they paly in the safety of the crowd and it is also clear from recent litigation that the audience members are more and more likely to sue an artist if they perceive that it is the fault of the artist that they have been injured.

One other interesting conclusion from the study is that pressure is directly proportional to musical tempo. The faster the artist plays or the tempo of the music the more pressure is caused in the crowd. This is also directly proportional to the behaviour of the crowd which seems to increase in activity with those faster tempo artists. For example, moshing and skanking is rife amongst fans of punk and the forward and outward acceleration of the crowd add to the pressure.

A new phenomena which is believed to reduce the pressure on the primary barrier at concerts is the development of the Golden Circle. However far from reducing the pressure on the primary barrier this practice may in fact increase the pressure at this point. From research carried out earlier in this book and from photographic evidence from helicopters above the pit at concerts where the Golden Circle is used it is clear that the pressure at the secondary barrier is extremely high. Although this has not been measured by the pressure barrier it is evident from the crowd density shown in the aerial photographs. The only actual benefit of the Golden Circle is to decrease the pressure on the primary barrier. However as the participants inside the Golden Circle are not those most heavily affiliated to the band nor those who practice the cultural behaviour associated with the band then the idea of the Golden Circle does not work to best effect. Those in the Golden Circle are there because they pay a premium price rather than because they are the most vociferous supporters. In questionnaires to those outside the Golden Circle at a recent event, 88% of those interviewed (2000) did not know that by not purchasing tickets for the Golden Circle they would end up at least 35 metres away from the artist. If the Golden Circle were employed effectively and efficiently then it would be an excellent way to reduce pressure at the primary barrier, however as can be seen by the example of Roskilde, only 550 people at one event can create as much pressure as a crowd of 75,000 at another.

It is clear that a great deal of work still needs to be carried out in this area and it will be many years before a definitive answer to the problem of crowd pressure and density is clearly identified. However this preliminary experiment has made a start on the road to identifying and eradicating such issues at events.

It must be noted that in this chapter the main focus of the work has not been to discredit the use of the single barrier system, the work has been to focus on changes in barrier design and usage and to see if these changes have any pertinent information which could make the use of a single barrier system more efficient and effective.

6 PAN EUROPEAN HEALTH & SAFETY ISSUES

The identification across Europe of some of the most pertinent health and safety factors and crowd management issues is one of the most important ways to create an overview of the management of the pan-European event industry. To identify these issues a series of seminars were held in Berlin and Groningen to identify from a collective of European festival event promoters, producers and managers what major issues needed to be addressed to enhance a greater harmony across European festivals and events.

One of the most difficult issues facing an event organiser is the identification of the type or types of attendee that will be visiting an event. A crowd consists of a large number of individuals who meld into groups of attendees when in contact with others visiting an event. Some may be non-participatory in much of the behaviour exhibited at a concert, some will be highly focused on the

Crowd at Roskilde Festival.

event for a range of reasons. Other attendees will mimic those taking part in the event whilst some may actively seek out dangerous activities through which they can achieve their sense of belonging to a group or an event.

Many types of behaviour are participatory but often such behaviour can become aggressive or hostile. It is also clear however that the majority of behaviour is in harmony with the event and thus expressive and fun. This chapter will mix the physical presence of the crowd with the psychological, social and cultural diversity found across the European festival event scene. It can also be deduced from the aforementioned research that there are a wide range of catalysts which produce the crowd dynamics associated with an event. These range from the actions of both internal and external customers to socio-cultural, climatic and physical site factors which the organiser has little or no control over. Thus it is clear that the tensions at such events are caused by the relationship model shown below.

Although this model is driven by extraneous factors including crowd size, genre of music, length of the event and demographics, it is clear that the reduction of such a model to four main factors gives clarity to this chapter. The first part of this chapter deals with health and safety issues across Europe whilst the second part focuses on the climate and its effects on the concert environment.

Internal Customer Relations	Socio-Cultural/ Psychological Factors
External Customer Relations	Physical Factors (Climate/ Environment)

Health & Safety Issues

Introduction

The first issue which was identified by those taking part in the seminars was the differing ways in which health and safety was viewed and implemented at venues across Europe. However, it was clear from those at the seminars that very little behaviour was specific to a particular venue at a specific event and most behavioural aspects encountered at concerts relating to the area of health and safety were generic across Europe. There were a small number of differences in the behaviour encountered but these incidences tended to be linked to musical genre and the way in which the cultural and social norms and values of the audiences in different countries reacted to certain genres of music and the differing contexts within which such genres were viewed.

One important piece of evidence which led to the development of the statement in the previous paragraph was the identification of a number of concerts which identified themselves as pan-European and drew a substantial audience from outside of their own country. It was ascertained that the behaviour of the crowd at such gatherings was fairly uniform and that apart from language difficulties and small cultural and behavioural differences the audience and their view of health and safety was fairly uniform. From previous research at two of these festivals (Roskilde and Nijmegen) it became clear that the way in which the audience behaved, what they wore and the demographics ascertained were fairly uniform in nature. It can also be seen from the research carried out at these concerts and others across Europe that the majority of health and safety incidences which troubled the concert organisers were often focused on the campsite rather than the event arena.

There seems to be a correlation between the control exerted on the campsite and the lack of apparent control exerted in camping areas, where the more controlled environment has less problematic incidences than the area which is less tightly controlled and monitored. It is clear that many of the problems at the forefront of concert organisers in Europe are those related to fire and the recent development of rituals where the campers set their belongings alight plus any rubbish on the site on the last night of the concert or festival.

The creation of smaller, more manageable campsite areas has reduced the tendency to set large fires on the last night of the event and also the timing of event finishes. Extending the activities of those camping on site to the early hours of the morning has tended to relieve the boredom and to extend the feeling of community and thus through careful management of the issue at these events, fire and other final night problems can be avoided or at least reduced. From those attending the Berlin seminars it became apparent that as behaviour changes at events the spread of such behaviour very quickly becomes pan-European. This phenomenon was identified by organisers as one caused by the will to travel across Europe to events as cheaper air fairs, open camp sites and an abundance of events became a reality. It only takes one attendee to show others what has happened at an event elsewhere in Europe or to even post pictures on one of the many event websites to generate behavioural patterns which create a consistent event environment which spreads the length and breadth of Europe. In such cases good practice is often difficult to disseminate as so many poor practices are enjoyed by the audience because such practices break the hold of the organiser on the developing society of the event. As we are now in the grip of an internal culture of safety and all of the constraints which accompany it we tend to forget that the external customers create situations which very often fall outside the control systems which we create. In these cases the utilisation of fluid risk and hazard strategies are key elements in the neutralising of the dangers that some of these practices present.

Alcohol and Drug Related Issues

No matter which event is visited across Europe, alcohol and drugs or lack of them is a constant reminder of what drives behaviour in crowds. Alcohol and drug usage is widespread across Europe but seems to be related in different ways to specific genres of music. Although alcohol is an ever-present accompaniment to music festivals, or not if the case in point is straight-edge, drugs are often genre-specific related to the sub-culture supported by, or supporting the genre. For example concert organisers across Europe have identified punk and hip-hop as the two musical genres where the drug problem is the greatest. Historically genres such as dance and its relationship to ecstasy were possibly the best documented with the creation of a 'moral panic' caused by the media around the reported dangers of its ingestion. With each new, reinvented, revitalised or historic genre an individual or series of drugs can be identified. The culture of alcohol and drug abuse across Europe does differ from country to country with exceptional problems identified in Scotland and the Netherlands. The type of drugs identified and the frameworks in place to deal with the issues surrounding them are not dissimilar across Europe. Some countries such as the Netherlands are very pro-counselling and provide drug substitutes as well as legalising some drugs to alleviate a range of problems occurring at concert venues not only through the taking of substances but also through the selling of drugs at events.

The use of glass is banned at many concerts in the UK and in some other European countries. At concerts in Switzerland glass has not been banned and the incidents involving dangerous activities utilising glass at events are minimal. The organisers of the festivals in Switzerland where glass containers are allowed identify the educational aspect and the way in which their events are managed as key reasons for this. The promoters from Switzerland identified the genre of music and the type of behaviour expected at the concerts as other reasons to why glass in this context does not seem to cause danger. However, it was the norm in other European countries to ban the use of glass and bottles as the danger caused to others was extremely high.

Issues with Musical Genre

Differing musical genre was identified by the organisers as a focus of research. There were representatives from across Europe dealing with a wide range of genres from dance, through heavy metal to classical. Although there were some individual or isolated incidents in many genres it was clear that only one genre troubled the majority of those organising events. It was established almost exclusively that the only genre highlighted where it was perceived that violent behaviour was an issue was that associated with the genre of hip-hop. The culture and behaviour of the crowd at such events was identified as anti-social and difficult to deal with. Although the behaviour can be easily managed the concert organisers felt that dealing with the culture surrounding the genre as well as the musicians and fans themselves was an extremely difficult job.

Dealing with Crowd Behaviour

The behaviour of the crowd at the front of stage differed from country to country and from genre to genre. It is clear that the British crowd is by far the most boisterous and that dealing with their behaviour needs a much more creative management strategy than most places in Europe. The use of barriers as a crowd controlling mechanism differs across Europe and the emphasis placed on the barrier ranges from essential to not needed across the event spectrum. However, the utilisation of the barrier is related to a series of management strategies and it was identified that these strategies are essential in the management of the crowd at all events whether barriers were used as deterrents or for the control and sectioning of the crowd.

It is evident that many European concerts have a strong advanced and concert day communication strategy that identifies to those attending the event what behaviour is expected at the concert venue. In many cases behaviour which is not acceptable is also identified and the communication stategy employed

Crowd management and audience interface at the barrier at Reading Festival.

is often deterrent enough to enable a more efficient management of the audience on access, during the concert through to egress. It is evidenced in the research that many European concert organisers tolerate less informal behaviour at concerts than organisers in the UK. In some cases this owes its origins to specific problems and issues and in others it is to enable the exertion of control to a situation which from knowledge and past experience can cause issues to arise at any time. There are of course different ways of dealing with such behaviour and it must be noted that to reduce the options for crowd anti-social behaviour at events in the UK may have an adverse affect on crowd attendance at festivals and events. It is this conundrum which faces many events organisers across Europe. When is an event safe and when is an event too safe if there is ever such a situation? In reality the question is can an event ever be too safe taking into consideration all of the issues which can occur during the life of an event?

The planning and execution of operational, tactical and strategic systems has been very successful across Europe. In many cases spotters are employed at the operational level to assist stewards and supervisors with spotting problems or issues within a crowd. Tactical awareness has been employed at management and supervisory level whilst the management team has delivered strong strategic leadership in the creation of a framework within which all of those employed can work. This type of planning has been very successful across Europe. A decade ago when the behaviour of a crowd towards an artist was seen as violent or extreme other venues on the tour would put in maximum security and crowd management plans to ensure that they were ready for the same or similar behaviour. However, more often than not the cultural inferences at the one event were not transferred to other events on the tour and thus companies wasted valuable time and effort in preparing for the worst case. Over the past decade as communication systems have become more advanced and crowd management specialists more aware of this type of reaction and the need for an immediate reflexive response no longer exists as contingencies are already in place in case such problems occur. As we move forward in time more uniform structures will be created, which in turn will enable not just the audience but the workers and artists to understand the expectation of the event or festival in any location.

Artist Behaviour and the Effect it has on Crowd Behaviour

One area identified by all operators at the seminars which causes a great deal of controversy in Europe is the way in which bands behave on stage. The behaviour of an artist in front of a crowd can incite the audience to change or modify their behaviour to a more dangerous level. Incidents of artists inciting the crowd are manifold and have in some cases ended with other members of the audience targeting particular people and causing actual harm to them. The obverse of this is where an artist controls the audience so that danger is averted. One prime example of this is the 1995 tour across Europe by Green Day, where the artist played a two-hour set but only 55 minutes of the set was dedicated to music. The rest of the set was building up and calming down the audience. Where an artist has such control of the audience the job of the crowd managers can be almost eliminated or at any rate reduced.

A worrying development identified in five European countries last year was that of lateral pushing, first from stage right and then from stage left. This action results in audience becoming destabilised which can cause them to fall, if pushed or slip, if a sudden gap opens. This may then cause possible trampling or crowd collapse. Artists are well aware of the dangers of lateral movements and to condone and incite such behaviour does cause concert organisers a number of concerns. The crowd managers already have enough problems to deal with when audience member are crowd surfing without the added pressures of focusing on others falling to the ground or being crushed by those following a type of behaviour initiated by the artist.

The MC or the front person in a band has a great deal of influence on the crowd and this can be seen in incidences with Pearl Jam and The Red Hot Chilli Peppers where the actions of the artist assist in the safety of the crowd or impact on the incident occurring. Unfortunately there have over the past few years been a number of incidences where artists have incited the crowd whilst an incident is in progress or whilst the crowd managers are trying to deal with such incidents.

The Missile Throwing Culture

Aggressive behaviour in the crowd is becoming more prevalent at festivals across Europe and the throwing of objects onto the stage has caused a number of accidents and curtailments of shows. Often such acts are misinterpreted by the artist or the audience and as such the often fragile audience/artist relationship is compromised. The main incidences of missile throwing are caused by boredom or lack of communication. Bottle wars and missile throwing often occur between artists when the experience of the audience dips below an acceptable level and the audience look to other elements to keep them occupied and amused. The throwing of urine in bottles is unsavoury but often seen as an everyday occurrence where an audience know no better as this is their only experience of an event. It is therefore important to coach the first time concertgoers about behaviour and what will happen in the concert environment.

Genre Predictability

Audiences watching many genres of music are very predictable. For all of its alternativeness, punk is extremely predictable. What the audience will wear, how they dance and how they behave is easily predicted well before the show takes place. The posturing, the attitude and the accompanying behaviour are all well documented and can be easily dealt with by the crowd managers. Hip-hop however and anomalies like the Oasis audience are another matter and often the unpredictability of the violent behaviour of both artists and audience can cause a strain on the management of such events. The one real way to meet this challenge is firstly to create a sound fluid risk assessment, analysis and management structure. By the development of such a framework all eventualities are being catered for. Secondly, it is important to create a profiling history across Europe of artists and their behaviour. This will then allow concert organisers to have a better and more reliable picture of an artist or an event to ensure that what they are planning fits with the audience behavioural patterns that have been collected over a period of time. Focusing on research which took place on the last Oasis tour it became apparent that the main focus of the audience was not on the music of the artist but on three other elements as well these which were drinking, football and the craic. Where the crowd manager has differing foci in the audience then their job becomes so much harder. In the case of hip hop the focus on gang and gun culture is very prevalent and thus the difficulties in the management of the event are magnified.

Mixed Genre Management
One of the most difficult types of crowd to control is a mixed genre crowd. In cases where the audience is self-selecting for each artist on stage or where the overall genre is similar but different artists are appearing the control of the audience is less difficult. However at an event where you have a wide range of non-compatible artists with no other outlet for the crowd other than a single stage there will be problems. Thus the total experience of the crowd is essential to enable an event to go off without incident. Many more concerts today provide a range of youth cultural activities to keep the audience amused. These range from fairground rides to half pipes and from dry skiing to cinema. Thus the experience cycle is broken up by a range of activities giving the attendee a purpose for attending and making them less likely to exert anti-social behaviour to other attendees.

Ingress and Egress
Another element identified by event organisers across Europe which causes major health and safety problems is ingress and egress. If thousands of people arrive at the same time at a festival site and the capacity to deal with the audience numbers is not planned then there will be serous problems for the organisers. Ingress gates must have enough lanes to deal with easy access flow and there must be the capacity to increase these gates if necessary. Secondly, unlike many festivals where audience members camp on the last night, the one-off or series of events must have the capacity to get rid of the audience effectively and efficiently at the end of the event. In many cases in the past

Queing lanes at Live 8 concert in Hyde Park.

this has not happened and extra transport and welfare has had to be drafted in to ensure that the audience can leave the site as effectively and efficiently as possible. Where this has not been possible communication systems should be in place to enable the audience to discover how they can achieve this. It is clear from many festival organisers that once the audience leave the show they perceive that this is the end of their responsibility. However, more and more non-effective and efficient egress and delivery of people to a safe destination to carry on with their journey is being frowned upon by those granting licences.

Difficulties When a Festival is Over

The most problematic time for festival organisers in Europe was identified as when the music stops. This is when the audience either leave or go back to campsites. When a festival closes if there is no further entertainment then people start to entertain each other. Often at such times, what is deemed acceptable behaviour turns into anti-social behaviour and tents, toilets and other temporary structures have been destroyed, burnt down or become part of a mass bonfire on the campsite. There are festivals and events in Europe where people travel specifically to cause trouble. At one such event in Finland which holds 20,000, 10,000 people congregate outside the area specifically to cause trouble. Although it is difficult to see into the festival, the fans can hear the music and there are excellent amenities as the festival is in a beauty spot which is part of a town/seaboard complex. Added to this is the tension between the audience and the figure of authority, namely the police. At this festival the major conflict comes when the police try to break up the sub festival and the audience then turn on the police and violence breaks out.

In the case of this festival two issues were addressed which alleviated the problems. Firstly the event finish was extended to 5am which then gave time for the crowd to be moved on early the next day without the problems of fire and boredom (this negated the internal problem with setting fire to toilets and tents). Secondly crowds were discouraged from visiting the sub-site very early on in the process and then turned away well away from the site if they did not have valid tickets. At the festival site the police presence was exchanged for that of friendly crowd management operatives which diffused the problems with authority.

The Psychology of the Crowd and the Modification of Their Behaviour

Communicating with the Audience

The creation of a communication system which gives the audience access to as much information as possible well in advance of the event is a key factor in enabling the audience to arrive at the event in clothes that suit the weather conditions and bringing with them a variety of elements that will enhance their enjoyment of the show such as sun cream, water, something to sit on and a hat.

Utilising the Profiling System

Although there are expected norms and values identified with genres of music and issues relating to the placement and timing of an event, the aforementioned profiling of the audience can also add a great deal of information to the communication strategy needed for the event.

Profiling the audience year on year builds up a focused demographic and behavioural representation of the type of audience who will be attending the event. From the audience profile the event organiser can build up an advanced picture of the audience and the likely behaviour of the audience attending. As well as this, buying patterns for bars, food and retail outlets can be ascertained to ensure that the stock control can be managed effectively. It is clear that if an artist or genre of music has been experiencing a pattern of behaviour which has caused issues on site the organiser is forewarned and thus they have the ability to start a risk programme from a point of informed delivery. If this is the case then such delivery will enable fine tuning to take place later on if a change in profile is detected. This fluidity of risk analysis and assessment can elicit change right up until the start of an event.

Website Utilisation

The website is crucial to the moulding of the way in which concert attendees behave prior to, during and after an event. It is important that the more complex the information, the simpler it is made on the website. The website is an extremely versatile medium used by a growing population of concertgoers as the only media viewed before an event. In research last year at six events throughout Europe 83% of those attending concerts stated that their only contact with the event was through a website. The website tool can be utilised educationally to ensure that the fist time concert goer is *au fait* with the site, the way to behave, what can be purchased, what to wear and health and safety matters pertaining to the event and the site. The way that the language on the site is used is essential. For example if it is too complex the average 13-18 year old will not understand, or worse not bother, to revisit the site for further details.

If the information required is not accessible within two clicks of the mouse then the concertgoer is likely to leave the site. The type of audience member who attends concerts utilises the site not only for information but also for special interest stories or reminders of past festivals. The more a site displays the more likely your communication strategy is to work. From past research it has been ascertained that for many internal customers the event starts with set up and finishes with the strike. However for the customer the experience may start with their own decision to purchase a ticket and end 20 years later when they stop talking to friends about it. Thus a website may be visited by people over a period of years not only for updates but also for nostalgia reasons.

Whilst identifying behavioural codes and other best practice it is essential to identify the sort of incidents that bad behaviour and practice has resulted in. This is more likely to have an effect on those reading. For example the Roskilde website identifies the tragedy and does not try to hide the past events. Thus the writers of the site can relate what has happened since and the type of management structures and best practice put in place to ensure that such an incident does not happen again. It is also important on websites not to use confusing, conflicting or ambiguous non user-friendly titles or text. For example, the usage of the word security instead of steward is often a bad move as security is an authority word whereas steward is a user-friendly word. Such small details can often diffuse situations in advance of a show. This may diffuse the hostile audience feelings and make for better relationships before, during and after the event.

Attitude and Experience

Following on from diffusing hostile relationships between the internal and external customer, attitude and experience are vital elements to an effective concert strategy. Just as reducing hostile language on the website is important so too are a number of cosmetic changes to events. One example of this is the changing of the colour of the T-shirt that crowd managers, spotters and stewards wear from black to a more friendly colour such as orange or red. This has been proved in a number of countries to diffuse a situation where the audience relate black to authority but relate orange or red to helpfulness. Such a change can modify the way in which the internal and external customers relate to each other.

The size and placing of signs in the auditorium is also important and the way in which the signs give information. A change to a user-friendly system is much better than bombarding everyone with information overload.

On Site Information

As has already been identified on-site information is vitally important. It is clear from European research that information should be well spread out and not confined just to a small number of places. First aid and other universal signs should be placed for maximum visibility from all areas within the event site. Exit and emergency signs also need to be highly visible and there must be nowhere within the site where one of these cannot be seen. The reason for this is that recent research shows that a large number of audience members site themselves where they are sure that they are in easy reach of an exit.

The way that an audience behaves tends to be related to the demographics. For example the younger concertgoers tend to try to get as close to the artist as possible (98% of under 18s at European festivals last year) whilst older concertgoers tend to identify where they are safest and will gravitate to these places to ensure that they can find a way out if necessary. Although this is a fairly general view, from research it is evident that different groups of people engage in different activities when visiting a concert or festival and it is these activities which are related to their primary reason for attending the event.

These lead the attendees to congregate at specific points in an arena when visiting a festival or event. It is also another reason why an advanced site map is important.

All attendees create a personal risk assessment when entering an event arena. The reason for this is so that they can ascertain how safe they are. All attendees have a mental checklist where they tick off a set of criteria which to them identifies that they will be safe in the event environment. Once this has been carried out the attendee will then practice their set of norms and values related to the event or genre. It is clear that the personal risk assessment of each attendee will vary to some extent and the prioritisation will be different from person to person. The risk management system therefore must contain all of the possible issues that the audience identify as 'safety factors' and more. The risk management strategy must also prioritise, however, the prioritisation of certain factors must not be seen to reduce others as such a move will make members of the audience unsettled. The key to a safe (psychologically) event is for the safety factors of the internal and external customers to create a matched set of values.

New Technologies

New technology has increased information access across Europe. Video screens or displays, websites, scoreboards, moving texts, text messaging and others have all decreased the time and distance between a sender and a receiver and audience and event. Both macro and micro communication has improved thus greatly negating excuses for poor communication systems at events and festivals. However, often such messages are encoded in such a way that only a select few concertgoers can decode the message. Hence such messages should be created so that they are simple in their origin and can be decoded by the maximum number of people to gain maximum effect.

Although exclusivity of access is a way of increasing sales it also reduces the effect and impact of a message to the general event populace. The specially encoded messages should only be used to inform all of the management or internal customers of problems within the festival or event which if universally decoded would cause mass panic within the auditorium. These special messages are also fast and simple to enable those managing the event to utilise the safest and most reliable systems to combat an emergency.

As well as utilising new technology, another effective tool utilised by those giving information through messaging systems is word of mouth. Although the message may sometimes lose its effect or be misinterpreted it is clear that word of mouth or face-to-face contact is essential to enable the concertgoer to clearly understand certain messages. For example a good MC is essential to a show. The MC has to be someone who is respected by the audience. For instance if the crowd is getting restless and the MC comes on stage to talk to them, the respect that the audience has can often diffuse a situation which may have got out of hand. The use of an MC also breaks up the monotony of a show. Many seasoned punters will not be satisfied with a constant stream of band-break-band-break-band but prefer to hear someone communication with them about gossip backstage and issues at the event. It is a kind of news broadcast. An event or festival is multi-layered and the way in which this layering works is to enable different types of audience member to access a wide range of networks within the event itself. At the lower layers, the interface with the event may just be functional and accessed through the artist playing and the existence at the event over a three-day period. At the higher levels, the access may be through a fan club, meeting the bands, accessing the latest releases and through relays back to blogs or writing for a student magazine. Thus the multi-layered nature of such events enables all to access at least one area of interest.

Key Factors in the Staging of an Event

It is common sense to assume that all event organisers realise the key factors which need to be put in place to enable an event to run more smoothly in the first instance. It is clear from European research that most organisers identify a fairly priced, total experience which is clear and well managed. As well as this those organising events in Europe identified a reduced garbage situation and a well decorated simple site as key initial factors in the development of an event. The way in which such events are constructed means that the additions and developments at these types of music events are efficiently and effectively managed. The utilisation of simple practices such as the lighting of areas where the concertgoer needs access and limiting the lighting in areas where access is prohibited are crucial in the creation of an efficiently managed festival or event. Many of the issues encountered today at festivals and events are the same as those encountered 25 years ago. Many of the ways of dealing with these issues are the simple ones used so many yeas ago but have not been bettered. Where a festival has been running for many years and the modification of systems has been seen. It is often the case that through trial and error the original systems have been put back in place, as they were the most effective.

The Site Map

The utilisation of a site map is one way of ensuring that attendees are *au fait* with the site. Many festivals across Europe provide a site map for every attendee. The map is attached to a lanyard and thus it fits around the neck of the attendee. Some sitemaps are too detailed or have misleading distances. A scale map with the key elements will suffice. Key elements that a site map must include are a lost point, bars, toilets, first aid and entrances and exits as well as stages. Accompanying this there should be an itinerary which informs the attendee of the artists, their timings and which stage they are appearing on. Without these few elements the day or festival period for an attendee can be a poor experience as they have to find out what is happening by exploration and trial and error where everything on the site is in relation to them.

The first part of this chapter has dealt with pan European health and safety issues focusing on the physical and psychological delivery of a safe, effective and efficient event. The second part of the chapter deals with the way in which climate can affect the event and how event organisers utilise a series of elements to help enhance the experience of those who fall foul of climate and event conditions.

Climate Issues at Events and Festivals

Climate issues at events and festivals are a burning topic across Europe at the present time. The greening of concerts and the awareness of what is happening to the climate throughout the world are at the forefront of the minds of both the organisers and those attending events. In recent years, high winds, lightning strikes, flooding and excessive heat have caused deaths and injury at concert events across Europe. In many cases event organisers have put contingency plans in progress to alleviate issues caused by adverse weather conditions; however, some are still wrestling with a number of concerns caused by quick changes in microclimates which directly affect their festivals or events.

Drinking Water and Issues Related to Excessive Heat and Sunlight

One of the major universal needs at concerts is the supply of drinking water and water for other uses. Storage tanks used for storing water for drinking and showers need to be able to cope with the volume required to meet the needs of attendees during extremes in temperatures often found at events. As the majority of events take place in the summer it is always hoped that the weather will be dry and that it is fairly hot and sunny. This type of concert environment is most conducive to the attendee. However from conversations with the police in several European countries at events such as soccer matches state that hot weather increases the drinking of alcohol before and after games and also increases violence towards individuals. As one police officer said: "If we have a violent game we pray for 'Mr Rain' as 'Mr Rain' dampens down the ardour of a crowd and they are less likely to cause trouble and drink less before a game."

Water Shortages

An example of an issue with drinking water can occur where a festival has a high average attendance for all three days of the event. The maximum capacity of the storage tanks is just enough to cope with the normal day-to-day needs of attendees. However the temperatures during the festival are in the 80s. This means that the call on water for drinking and showers will be greater and also the loss through convection and evaporation will increase the need for greater capacity. Thus a contingency plan is needed to ensure that extra water is on hand in case the original volume is fully utilised. A number of festivals across Europe have been caught out by an extra draw on water facilities. In the case of drinking water and other beverages the supply of water is essential owing to the climate during the summer. Allied to the heat of the sun is the creation of three other phenomena. The first is arid dust-blown conditions which cause dust irritation, dryness and sometimes dirt storms which make living on the campsite at events extremely difficult. However, by dampening down the site with water spray this can be alleviated. Again such a task needs good planning as dampening depends on water reserves for such practices. Heat and wind also causes dehydration in the audience where moisture caused by sweating is taken away from the body by dry wind. Once this moisture has been removed it is replaced by more moisture which gradually reduces the water content of the body and the onset of dehydration.

Sunburn

The second issue is sunburn. One of the key components of a concertgoer's survival pack should be sun cream. The onset of sunburn can cause dehydration, delirium, hyperthermia and nausea, vomiting and sunstroke. This condition is especially prevalent in those who are first time attendees who haven't sufficient knowledge to enable them to create a survival pack in advance of the show. One of the most common deficiencies in such a pack is correctly identified sun cream factor. If too low a factor is utilised in sun block treatment then the cream is still ineffective. Total application is also useful as clothing moves from time to time especially loose fitting dresses, skirts and vests. The areas around the eyes and inner arms and thighs are especially susceptible. It is also possible to get burned with cloud cover as sunlight (UV rays) penetrates through cloud.

Fire

The third issue is fire. Although fire has already been identified earlier in this chapter this section does not relate to man-made fire but that caused by excessive temperatures or a lightning strike. Fire is not a regular occurrence at events but can break out in a number of ways these include:

- Electrical fire from the PA or lighting rig
- Bush fire from surrounding parched vegetation
- Lightning strike
- Campsite fire from unattended fire plus wind
- Backstage fire in temporary structures

However, in this part of the chapter the focus will be on non-deliberate fire. This is more common in European countries where they have a hot climate all year round, Australia South America, the US and Africa. These sorts of fires are usually a combination of dry vegetation and either carelessness or deliberate action. The deliberate activity of setting tents or toilets alight is in this case far away from the usual cause. These fires are caused by a cooking fire getting out of hand, a careless cigarette or naked flames used for lighting purposes. What happens is that because of the dry ground and vegetation the fire spreads rapidly and can cause extensive damage not just to the concert site but also to surrounding vegetation, industry and accommodation in a wide area. Not only are such fires devastating to the site and the community but can cause mass panic at concerts. The nature of this type of fire is such that it is not well understood and its intensity, inconsistency and capacity to jump gaps means that it can be difficult to control. If the fire is combined with high winds it can cause mass devastation as it has the capacity to travel further.

Communication with the audience where such situations are likely is vital and a fire plan covering all eventualities and a very strong fluid evacuation plan and risk assessment need to be updated effectively and efficiently. It is also pertinent to have at least two contingency plans in operation owing to the unstable nature of a fire situation. Not only does the fire itself cause problems but the associated smoke can lead to injury and death through temporary blindness and/or asphyxiation. If smoke is present it will depend on the barometric pressure and the wind direction/force what instructions are given. In the case of evacuation, the safe place for evacuation may change at a moments notice and thus it is important to have sound communication systems to enable a quick change of plan, hence the contingency planning documentation.

Cold

Just as high temperatures are associated with heat stoke and hyperthermia, low temperatures are associated with hypothermia. In hot climates or on sunny days where lack of cloud cover lets in the heat and rays from the sun, in the evening a lack of cloud cover reduces the ability of the atmosphere to retain the day's heat. In Australia for example at night temperatures can reach near to freezing. As identified by the European organisers one key element associated with first aid at concerts on hot days are the number of people treated with cold-related illnesses. Many people are not aware owing to ignorance that at a concert when the sun goes down and you have only brought the vest and shorts that you arrived with, the temperature will drop. For the whole of the day the crowd has been dancing and moving to the bands and the warmth of the collective mass has caused the audience members to sweat and to lose fluid. In the evening as the crowd mass separates and the individual moves to the campsite or to go home they are hit by the drop in temperature. This drop causes shivering, which in turn causes the hairs on the body to stand up to try to preserve the warmth in and around the body. However if the attendee does not have sufficient clothing to restore some sort of heat balance the reaction of nature is to continue to try to save the surrounding heat. Eventually the body temperature will cool and then draw on the core temperature which will then also cool causing a hypothermic reaction. This reaction can send the body into the same kind of scenario which excessive heat causes. It is thus clear that education through communication and the website is essential to enable those visiting concerts to be sensible in what they wear and what they bring. It is also clear that some kind of helpline/helpdesk or welfare system is essential for those without this education and for those who are first time attendees who are not used to the concert environment or context.

Wind

Wind at a dry concert has been shown to spread fire, cause dust storms and to dehydrate. However, wind also has its positive elements as it can reduce temperatures on site. One key element in the monitoring of wind is to ensure that wind loading check equipment is in place before and during the show to ensure that there is not too much wind that may make the show and equipment unsafe. It is also important to ensure that this equipment is in use after the show to make safety checks before taking down the equipment.

Rain, Flooding and Land Use

Just as heat, fire and cold are elements caused by climate, so too is rain and flooding. Across Europe flooding on campsites is seen every year. Unfortunately there is no rhyme or reason to such occurrences and one year might bring torrential rain and the next a dust storm. The amount of mud and flooding is directly related to precipitation, soil type, drainage and bedrock coupled with former use of the land. One example of a difficult drainage area is Hyde Park, which has a concrete car park built underneath. When rainfall is high and outstrips drainage run-off the ground becomes extremely flooded and muddy.

Throughout Europe different concert and festival venues are built on different surfaces. These range from chalk, to limestone, to granite, to clay. Some events take place on well drained rich soils whilst others take place on poorly drained soils with no nutrients. The more nutrients the better the quality of vegetation although in some countries such as Greece, Spain and Italy very hardy shrubs and grasses grow in poor soils which can act as windbreaks and dust dampeners whilst succulents can act as barriers to the spread of fire. In the case of rich nutrient soils with limestone bedrock the benefit is twofold. The drainage is good and the soil composition conducive to the growing of strong healthy grass. In such cases heavy precipitation is well drained and the grass forms a layer which stops mud from forming giving a uniform well-drained site with little turf cut-up.

However, poorly drained soils in areas where there is granite bedrock with clay subsoil are prone to flooding and water logging. The dangers can be identified as follows:
- Decimation of camping grounds
- Thick mud which makes getting around the site difficult
- Contamination of water supplies
- Disease
- Traffic congestion
- Danger to electrical installations
- Suffocation and slippage

- Lack of dry areas to enable internal and external dry-out
- Reduction of dry space for those caught in the weather

All of the examples noted above come from sites around Europe and although rain and flooding does cause some problems in the arena the majority of problems are caused for those camping owing to the lack of drying out facilities and the way in which tents are pitched. It is also clear that at some festivals and events the camping grounds are the poorer, less well drained and often sloping areas of the site as these have little use for anything else.

In 2005 at the Glastonbury Festival severe flooding caused part of the camping grounds to be washed away which in turn stranded a large number of people without dry accommodation. Many of these people lost all of their belongings and spent the rest of the festival in a miserable state. Much was done to help and the cause of the flooding could not be identified in the risk assessment before the event as it was a one-off situation which had not happened previously.

Thick mud is another element which causes problems at an outdoor festival or event around Europe. The front of stage area is particularly susceptible to being churned up when rainfall is high. At many events where a nylon carpet is laid in front of stage this can act as a dampener for dust or a barrier for mud. However once water and mass crowds are place on top of such barriers it is only a temporary system as the churning of the feet of the crowd soon mix the carpet into the front of stage rain and soil.

Contamination and Disease

In a number of areas across Europe there have been incidences of contaminated water supplies where latrine water has become mixed with drinking water after a blowback in the system. Once this happens the drinking water cannot be used. It is interesting to note that because of this possibility many sites around Europe have hazard signs on water supplies and advocate that these cannot be used as drinking water just in case of contamination.

It was mentioned earlier in this chapter that Greenfield sites have a decontamination period of six weeks before an event. This is a safety system which is in place to try to minimise the possibility of the spread of disease especially where grazing animals have used the land previously. The six week period gives the organisers the time to rid the land of animal faeces, glass, barbed wire and other harmful substances as well as to carry out the requisite checks on drainage and previous usage.

Rainfall on faeces mixed into the soil can release bacteria which are harmful to those at the event. There is also the problem with tetanus which is found in the majority of soil samples. Thirdly the danger of sewage seepage into a site during heavy rain increases the possibility of diseases such as cholera and diphtheria. The danger arises where ground water is ingested, contact with broken skin occurs or rubbing eyes, ears or noses with contaminated hands. This usually occurs as a series of isolated incidents but the frequency often depends on the previous usage of the land or the severity of the flooding. It must be remembered here that disease can travel as easily in water as it does through the air and protective measures should be sought at all times. It is also useful to warn the concertgoers of the dangers albeit fairly remote that they would contract any of the accompanying diseases.

It is clear from research across Europe that people and transport do not mix and should be kept apart as much as possible. However, where flooding occurs, no matter how much boarding or straw is laid in car parks there will still be problems for those exiting a site. This inevitably causes congestion and thus what was hoped to be an easy egress from a site turns into a major operation. To cope with this tractors are used to pull out stranded cars. In some cases cranes have had to be used and welfare tents and a place for attendees to get food and beverages are essential. One way to combat flooding is to bring in trackway. However to carpet all car parks and roadways with trackway would not be economically viable.

The most dangerous combination at any event is electricity and water and all sites take special care to ensure that all cabling and electrical appliances are protected against rain and ground water. At Lollapalooza in the US two people were electrocuted on their way back to the campsite after the show as they stepped into a puddle. The puddle had a length of cabling which had been exposed by the constant movement of site traffic during the set up for the show. The danger from electricity comes in the fact that you cannot see it, you cannot hear it and you cannot smell it and thus if it is there it is usually a hidden danger.

Mud and water in any area of the event arena can cause slippage and suffocation. This is especially prevalent in the front of stage area. For indie, punk, grunge or metal bands where crowd surfing, pogoing or other behaviour where forward and backward or lateral movement is found the danger from slippage on a muddy surface is high. Modern footwear does not give a great deal of traction and fans can easily slip. In the case of a moving crowd once slippage occurs in these conditions it tends to cause a domino effect and this takes down large areas of the audience. In very wet and muddy conditions a fan falling face down with others on top in water can cause suffocation. In the case of many deaths at concerts the death is caused by pressure from both the front and rear of the chest cavity making it impossible to breathe. In this case the pressure is on the back of the person prone on the ground and the push down causes the possibility of the mouth and nose being below the water level. If this continues for a short period suffocation can occur.

In the case of flooding the biggest difficulty for those organising an event is finding enough dry space for all of those who have lost their tents, become wet through or very cold. All of those at the seminar stated that in such weather they would not have the capacity to house everyone that needed a dry space. It is clear that those without tents are the first priority as their home for the event has been destroyed. However welfare should be on standby to counsel people who are in difficulties and first aid should also be supplied for those suffering from the many and varied illnesses that the association with wet or water can bring.

Hailstorms and Lightning Strikes

Two other major issues which are anomalies but do occur are hailstorms and lightning. Hail can devastate a campsite and destroy tents and temporary demountable structures and lightning is a killer. At an airshow in Germany one member of the audience was killed, one seriously injured and a number of others taken to hospital after a lightning strike. A lightning strike is difficult to work around and the only preparation really is a constant weather update to ensure that if storms are heading towards the event. There are many conflicting pieces of advice about lightning strikes and it is a fallacy that they do not strike in the same place twice as that is what lightning conductors rely on. Some advice states that attendees should get under cover whilst other evidence states that attendees should go out into the open. From research it appears that the following advice should be heeded. Identify structures which may be hit by lightning and evacuate them, give clear information from the stage to people in the arena so that they can prepare for a storm. However it is difficult to prepare for a lighting storm and unfortunately people are attracted to storms and act like sheep following the largest group rather than taking heed of safety information.

Show Stop

One of the most contentious issues in concert and festival management is when or if to stop the show. It is clear from those attending the seminars that a show should only be stopped as a last resort and if there is imminent danger to either the external or internal customer. Owing to the stage/audience divide it is clear that the averting of a problem backstage is easier to deal with as those working in this area are professionals and trained to follow safety procedures. However when the problem impinges on the audience it is more problematic. Those at the seminar identified six scenarios when the show should be stopped these were:

- Electrical failure
- Crowd collapse
- Structural collapse
- Dangerous weather conditions
- Fire
- Terrorist report

However when it came to identifying who, when and why the show should be stopped and the steps which should be taken, this was a more difficult problem to solve. It is clear from the research that a named industry person/persons should be responsible for the show stop. The person/persons should be appointed well in advance of the show/tour, must be competent, respected and have access to all information and parties involved in the show to be able to carry out the actions required.

However, the main difficulty with the action of stopping a show is the judgement used to identify when a show should be stopped. This is because if a show is stopped too soon and the danger vanishes then the person responsible is seen as a liability. If the show is stopped too late and people die because of the action then again the person stopping the show takes the responsibility for their actions after the event.

The action of stopping the show has to be both an objective/informed and subjective/gut decision and thus the timing of the stop is a competency issue. Someone who is competent will have taken everything into consideration when making the decision and everyone working on the show has to trust their judgement. The key to the action is taking responsibility and this responsibility is based on relevant information from competent people of a decision which is backed up by procedure. The procedure is important and all of those involved in such a decision, for example on site and artist security must meet before the show to discuss the procedure to be used. The steps in such a procedure are simple. Identify the system to be used, make sure that the communication of the system is known by all of the relevant people involved. The key is clarity, as long as everyone agrees with the system and the way it is to be put in place then show stop operation should be simple.

The concept of the show stop has been the most difficult and most avoided issue in heath and safety at concerts. This has been for a wide range of reasons which are:

- Not wishing to upset the audience
- Not wishing to upset the artists
- Not wishing to invoke an evacuation procedure unless necessary
- Incurring time penalties (financial) for over running and thus curtailing the show
- Issues of health and safety

The onset of a physical issue is an easier focus for those stopping the show. However, psychological issues are much more difficult to contend with.

The diagram on the next page is the start of an important process which will hopefully make the idea of show stop an every day contingency trusted by all that work at events.

FURTHER READING

Frosdick, S and Walley, L (1999). **Sport & Safety Management**. Butterworth Heinemann

Hannam, C (1997) **An Introduction to Health and Safety Management for the Live Music Industry**. Production Services Association

Huntington, J (2000). **Control Systems for Live Entertainment**. Focal Press

Menear, P and Hawkins T (1988) **Stage Management and Theatre Administration**. Phaidon, Oxford

Vasey, J (1999). **Concert Sound and Lighting Systems (3rd Ed)**. Focal Press

HSE (2000) **Managing Crowds Safely**. A guide for organisers at events and venues

HSE (1999) **The Event Safety Guide**. A guide to health, safety and welfare at music and similar events. HSE, London.

Mullis, A & Oliphant, K (1997) **Torts** Macmillan Press, London

Brazier, M (1993) **Street on Torts** Butterworth Heinnemann London

Trespass and Protest: Policing under the Criminal Justice and Public Order Act 1994 Home Office Research Study 190 1998.

Institution of Structural Engineers (1999) **Temporary Demountable Structures**. Guidance on Design, Procurement and Use. ISE, London.

HSE (1999) **Safe Use of Lifting Equipment**. HSE, London.

HMSO (1999) **Guide to Safety at Sports Grounds**. Fourth edition. HMSO, London

Wertheimer P. (1980) **Crowd Management** *Report of the Task Force on Crowd Control and Safety*. City of Cincinnati.

HMSO (1989) **The Hillsborough Stadium Disaster. Interim report** HMSO, London.

John J. Fruin, (1993) **The Causes and Prevention of Crowd Disasters**. (Originally presented at the First International Conference of Engineering for Crowd Safety, London).

Anthony DeBarros, (2000) **Concertgoers push injuries to high levels**. Published in USA Today, August 8th, 2000.

Au, S.Y.Z., Ryan, M.C., Carey, M.S. (1993) **Key principles in ensuring crowd safety in public venues**. In: Smith, R.A., Dickie, J.F. (eds.) *Engineering for Crowd Safety*, Amsterdam. Elsevier Science Publishers.

Au, S.Y.Z., Ryan, M.C., Carey, M.S., Whalley, S.P. (1993) **Managing crowd safety in public venues: a study to generate guidance for venue owners and enforcing authority inspectors**. HSE Contract Research Report No. 53/1993, London: HMSO.

Department of the Environment Advisory Committee on Pop Festivals (1973) **Pop Festivals Report and Code of Practice**. London: HMSO.

Dubin, G.H. (1974) **Medical care at large gatherings: a manual based on experiences in rock concert medicine**. U.S. Department of Health Education and Welfare

Hanna, J.A. (1995) **Emergency preparedness guidelines for mass, crowd-intensive events**. Emergency Preparedness Canada.

Home Office Emergency Planning College (1992) **Lessons learned from crowd-related disasters**. Easingwold Papers No.4, Easingwold: Emergency Planning College.

Leiba, T. (1999) **Crisis intervention theory and method**. In: Tomlinson, D., Allen, K. (eds.) *Crisis Services and Hospital Crises: mental health at a turning point*. Aldershot: Ashgate.

NHS (1999) **National Service Framework for Mental Health - modern standards and service models**. London: Department of Health.

Turner, B.A., Pidgeon, N.F. (1997) **Man-made disasters**. 2nd Edition. Oxford. Butterworth Heinemann.

Ackroyd, S. & Hughes, J. (1992) **Data Collection in Context**. 2nd ed. Essex: Longman Group UK Limited.

Ambrose, J. (2001) **The Violent World of Moshpit Culture**. [s.l.]: Omnibus Press.

Bell, J. (1996) **Doing Your Research Project: a guide for first-time researchers in education and social science**. 2nd ed. Buckingham: Open University Press.

Bignell, J. (1997) **Media Semiotics: an introduction**. Manchester: Manchester University Press.

Bilton. T. *et al.* (1996) **Introductory Sociology**. 3rd ed. Hampshire: Macmillan Press Ltd.

Bowdin, G. *et al* (2001) **Events Management**. Oxford: Butterworth-Heinemann.

Collins (2002) **Dictionary & Thesaurus**. Glasgow: HarperCollins Publishers.

Collins, M. & Cooper, I. (eds.) (1998) **Leisure Management: issues and applications**. Oxon: CAB International.

Crozier, W. (2000) **Music and Social Influence**. In: Hargreaves, D. & North, A. (eds.) *The Social Psychology of Music*. Oxford: Oxford University Press.

Davidson, J. (2000) **The Social in Music Performance**. In: Hargreaves, D. & North, A. (eds.) *The Social Psychology of Music*. Oxford: Oxford University Press.

Frosdick, S. (1997) **Managing Risk in Public Assembly Facilities**. In: Frosdick, S. & Walley, L. (eds.) *Sport and Safety Management*. Oxford: Butterworth-Heinemann.

Grainger-Jones, B. (1999) **Managing Leisure**. Oxford: Butterworth:Heinemann.

Hamm, C. (1995) **Putting Popular Music in its Place**. Cambridge: Cambridge University Press.

Haralambos, M. & Holborn, M. (1995) **Sociology Themes and Perspectives**. 4th ed. London: Collins Educational.

Hargreaves, D. & North, A. (eds.) (2000) **The Social Psychology of Music**. Oxford: Oxford University Press.

Health & Safety Executive (1999) **The Event Safety Guide: a guide to health, safety and welfare at music and similar events**. [s.l.]: HSE Books.

Highmore, M. (1997) **Safety Risks in Stadia and Sports Grounds**. In: Frosdick, S. & Walley, L. (eds.) *Sport and Safety Management*. Oxford: Butterworth-Heinemann.

Kemp, C. (2000) **Music Industry Management & Promotion**. 2nd ed. Huntingdon: ELM Publications.

Kraus, R. & Curtis, J. (1990) **Creative Management in Recreation, Parks, and Leisure Services**. 5th ed. Missouri: Times Mirror/Mosby College Publishing.

Longhurst, B. (1995) **Popular Music & Society**. Cambridge: Polity Press.

Mason, J. (1996) **Qualitative Researching**. London: SAGE Publications Ltd.

May, T. (1998) **Social Research: issues, methods and process**. 2nd ed. Buckingham: Open University Press.

Meltzer, R. (1987) **The Aesthetics of Rock**. New York: Da Capo Press.

Negus, K. (1996) **Popular Music in Theory: an introduction**. Cambridge: Polity Press.

Punch, K. (1998) **Introduction to Social Research: quantitative & qualitative approaches**. London: SAGE Publications Ltd.

Rogers, *et al.* (1995) **Social Psychology: a critical agenda**. Cambridge: Blackwell Publishers Inc.

Shuker, R. (1994) **Understanding Popular Music**. London: Routledge.

Silverman, D. (2000) **Doing Qualitative Research: a practical handbook**. London: SAGE Publications.

Smith, P. & Bond, M. (1998) **Social Psychology Across Cultures**. 2nd ed. Hertfordshire: Prentice Hall Europe.

Still, K. (1998)

Torkildsen, G. (1999) **Leisure and Recreation Management**. 4th ed. London: E & FN Spon.

Warne, C. (1997) **Crowd Risks in Sports Grounds**. In: Frosdick, S. & Walley, L. (eds.) *Sport and Safety Management*. Oxford: Butterworth-Heinemann.

Waters, I. (1994) **Entertainment, Arts and Cultural Services**. 2nd ed. Essex: Longman Group UK Ltd.

Web references

Barron, J. (1994) **Are the Kids Alright?: moshing tragedies abound at recent rock shows**. [online]. Available from: http://www.poprocks.com/journ/mosh.htm [Accessed 21 November 2002].

BBC (2002) **Promoters to Blame for Fan's Death say Limp Bizkit's Manager**. [online]. Available from: http://www.bbc.co.uk/radio1/artist_area/limpbizkit/ [Accessed 8 October 2002].

Crowd Dynamics [n.d.] **Crowd Management Information**. [online]. Available from: http://www.crowddynamics.com/Main/Crowd%20Control.htm [Accessed 15 November 2002].

Crowd Management Strategies (2001) **The Rock and Roll Wall of Shame**. [online]. Available from: http://www.crowdsafe.com/thewall.html [Accessed 15 November 2002].

Crowd Management Strategies (2002) **Mosher Friendly Guidelines**. [online]. Available from: http://www.crowdsafe.com/mosh.html [Accessed 10 October 2002].

Dotmusic (2000) **Concert Safety Investigated After Roskilde**. [online]. Available from: http://www.dotmusic.com/news/july2000/news14555.asp [Accessed 15 November 2002].

Dotmusic (2000) **Moshing Too Dangerous for Festivals**. [online]. Available from: http://www.dotmusic.com/news/July2000/news14443.asp [Accessed 17 October 2002].

Dotmusic (2000) **Roskilde Tragedy**. [online]. Available from: http://www.dotmusic.com/news/July2000/news14421.asp [Accessed 8 October 2002].

Goodwin, S. [n.d.] **An Evaluation of Crowd Safety Management and Controls Deployed for 'Mosh Pits' at Rock Concerts**. [online]. Available from: http://www.livemusiceducation.com/crowd%20surfing.htm [Accessed 8 October 2002].

Malavenda, P. (1995) **Moshing: Freedom of Expression or Liability?** [online]. Available from: http://www.geocities.com/Heartland/Village/3335/Moshing.htm [Accessed 21 November 2002].

Roadogz (2002) **Crowd Management @ BDO in Aussie**. [online]. Available from: http://www.roadogz.com/stories/downunder/crowdmanagement.htm [Accessed 17 October 2002].

Upton, M. [n.d.] **Risk Assessment for Casual Rock Concert Events**. [online]. Available from: http://www.crowddynamics.com/Concert%20Risks.htm [Accessed 1 October 2002].

Websites

www.dotmusic.com
www.crowdsafe.com
www.crowddynamics.com
www.glastonburyfestivals.co.uk
www.festivalnews.com
www.ilmc.com

ENTERTAINMENT TECHNOLOGY PRESS

FREE SUBSCRIPTION SERVICE

Keeping Up To Date with

Case Studies in Crowd Management

Entertainment Technology titles are continually up-dated, and all major changes and additions are listed in date order in the relevant dedicated area of the publisher's website. Simply go to the front page of www.etnow.com and click on the BOOKS button. From there you can locate the title and be connected through to the latest information and services related to the publication.

The author of the title welcomes comments and suggestions about the book and can be contacted by email at: ckemp01@bcuc.ac.uk

Titles Published by Entertainment Technology Press

ABC of Theatre Jargon *Francis Reid* **£9.95** ISBN 1904031099
This glossary of theatrical terminology explains the common words and phrases that are used in normal conversation between actors, directors, designers, technicians and managers.

Aluminium Structures in the Entertainment Industry *Peter Hind* **£24.95**
ISBN 1904031064
Aluminium Structures in the Entertainment Industry aims to educate the reader in all aspects of the design and safe usage of temporary and permanent aluminium structures specific to the entertainment industry – such as roof structures, PA towers, temporary staging, etc.

AutoCAD – A Handbook for Theatre Users *David Ripley* **£24.95** ISBN 1904031315
From 'Setting Up' to 'Drawing in Three Dimensions' via 'Drawings Within Drawings', this compact and fully illustrated guide to AutoCAD covers everything from the basics to full colour rendering and remote plotting.

Basics – A Beginner's Guide to Lighting Design *Peter Coleman* **£9.95** ISBN 1904031412
The fourth in the author's 'Basics' series, this title covers the subject area in four main sections: The Concept, Practical Matters, Related Issues and The Design Into Practice. In an area that is difficult to be difinitive, there are several things that cross all the boundaries of all lighting design and it's these areas that the author seeks to help with.

Basics – A Beginner's Guide to Special Effects *Peter Coleman* **£9.95** ISBN 1904031331
This title introduces newcomers to the world of special effects. It describes all types of special effects including pyrotechnic, smoke and lighting effects, projections, noise machines, etc. It places emphasis on the safe storage, handling and use of pyrotechnics.

Basics – A Beginner's Guide to Stage Lighting *Peter Coleman* **£9.95** ISBN 190403120X
This title does what it says: it introduces newcomers to the world of stage lighting. It will not teach the reader the art of lighting design, but will teach beginners much about the 'nuts and bolts' of stage lighting.

Basics: A Beginner's Guide to Stage Management *Peter Coleman* **£7.95**
ISBN 9781904031475
The fifth in Peter Coleman's popular 'Basics' series, this title provides a practical insight into, and the definition of, the role of stage management. Further chapters describe Cueing or 'Calling' the Show (the Prompt Book), and the Hardware and Training for Stage Management. This is a book about people and systems, without which most of the technical equipment used by others in the performance workplace couldn't function.

Basics – A Beginner's Guide to Stage Sound *Peter Coleman* **£9.95** ISBN 1904031277
This title does what it says: it introduces newcomers to the world of stage sound. It will not teach the reader the art of sound design, but will teach beginners much about the background to sound reproduction in a theatrical environment.

Building Better Theaters *Michael Mell* **£16.95** 1904031404
A title within our Consultancy Series, this book describes the process of designing a theater,

from the initial decision to build through to opening night. Michael Mell's book provides a step-by-step guide to the design and construction of performing arts facilities. Chapters discuss: assembling your team, selecting an architect, different construction methods, the architectural design process, construction of the theater, theatrical systems and equipment, the stage, backstage, the auditorium, ADA requirements and the lobby. Each chapter clearly describes what to expect and how to avoid surprises. It is a must-read for architects, planners, performing arts groups, educators and anyone who may be considering building or renovating a theater.

Close Protection – The Softer Skills *Geoffrey Padgham* **£11.95** ISBN 1904031390
This is the first educational book in a new 'Security Series' for Entertainment Technology Press, and it coincides with the launch of the new 'Protective Security Management' Foundation Degree at Buckinghamshire Chilterns University College (BCUC). The author is a former full-career Metropolitan Police Inspector from New Scotland Yard with 27 years' experience of close protection (CP). For 22 of those years he specialised in operations and senior management duties with the Royalty Protection Department at Buckingham Palace, followed by five years in the private security industry specialising in CP training design and delivery. His wealth of protection experience comes across throughout the text, which incorporates sound advice and exceptional practical guidance, subtly separating fact from fiction. This publication is an excellent form of reference material for experienced operatives, students and trainees.

A Comparative Study of Crowd Behaviour at Two Major Music Events
Chris Kemp, Iain Hill, Mick Upton **£7.95** ISBN 1904031250
A compilation of the findings of reports made at two major live music concerts, and in particular crowd behaviour, which is followed from ingress to egress.

Copenhagen Opera House *Richard Brett and John Offord* **£32.00** ISBN 1904031420
Completed in a little over three years, the Copenhagen Opera House opened with a royal gala performance on 15th January 2005. Built on a spacious brown-field site, the building is a landmark venue and this book provides the complete technical background story to an opera house set to become a benchmark for future design and planning. Sixteen chapters by relevant experts involved with the project cover everything from the planning of the auditorium and studio stage, the stage engineering, stage lighting and control and architectural lighting through to acoustic design and sound technology plus technical summaries.

Electrical Safety for Live Events *Marco van Beek* **£16.95** ISBN 1904031285
This title covers electrical safety regulations and good pracitise pertinent to the entertainment industries and includes some basic electrical theory as well as clarifying the "do's and don't's" of working with electricity.

The Exeter Theatre Fire *David Anderson* **£24.95** ISBN 1904031137
This title is a fascinating insight into the events that led up to the disaster at the Theatre Royal, Exeter, on the night of September 5th 1887. The book details what went wrong, and the lessons that were learned from the event.

Fading Light – A Year in Retirement *Francis Reid* **£14.95** ISBN 1904031358
Francis Reid, the lighting industry's favourite author, describes a full year in retirement. "Old age is much more fun than I expected," he says. Fading Light describes visits and

experiences to the author's favourite theatres and opera houses, places of relaxation and re-visits to scholarly intitutions.

Focus on Lighting Technology *Richard Cadena* **£17.95** ISBN 1904031145
This concise work unravels the mechanics behind modern performance lighting and appeals to designers and technicians alike. Packed with clear, easy-to-read diagrams, the book provides excellent explanations behind the technology of performance lighting.

Health and Safety Aspects in the Live Music Industry *Chris Kemp, Iain Hill* **£30.00** ISBN 1904031226
This title includes chapters on various safety aspects of live event production and is written by specialists in their particular areas of expertise.

Health and Safety Management in the Live Music and Events Industry *Chris Hannam* **£25.95** ISBN 1904031307
This title covers the health and safety regulations and their application regarding all aspects of staging live entertainment events, and is an invaluable manual for production managers and event organisers.

Hearing the Light – 50 Years Backstage *Francis Reid* **£24.95** ISBN 1904031188
This highly enjoyable memoir delves deeply into the theatricality of the industry. The author's almost fanatical interest in opera, his formative period as lighting designer at Glyndebourne and his experiences as a theatre administrator, writer and teacher make for a broad and unique background.

An Introduction to Rigging in the Entertainment Industry *Chris Higgs* **£24.95** ISBN 1904031129
This book is a practical guide to rigging techniques and practices and also thoroughly covers safety issues and discusses the implications of working within recommended guidelines and regulations.

Let There be Light – Entertainment Lighting Software Pioneers in Interview *Robert Bell* **£32.00** ISBN 1904031242
Robert Bell interviews a distinguished group of software engineers working on entertainment lighting ideas and products.

Lighting for Roméo and Juliette *John Offord* **£26.95** ISBN 1904031161
John Offord describes the making of the Vienna State Opera production from the lighting designer's viewpoint – from the point where director Jürgen Flimm made his decision not to use scenery or sets and simply employ the expertise of LD Patrick Woodroffe.

Lighting Systems for TV Studios *Nick Mobsby* **£45.00** ISBN 1904031005
Lighting Systems for TV Studios, now in its second edition, is the first book specifically written on the subject and has become the 'standard' resource work for studio planning and design covering the key elements of system design, luminaires, dimming, control, data networks and suspension systems as well as detailing the infrastructure items such as cyclorama, electrical and ventilation. Sensibly TV lighting principles are explained and some history on TV broadcasting, camera technology and the equipment is provided to help set the scene! The second edition includes applications for sine wave and distributed dimming, moving lights, Ethernet and new cool lamp technology.

Lighting Techniques for Theatre-in-the-Round *Jackie Staines* **£24.95**
ISBN 1904031013
Lighting Techniques for Theatre-in-the-Round is a unique reference source for those working
on lighting design for theatre-in-the-round for the first time. It is the first title to be published
specifically on the subject, it also provides some anecdotes and ideas for more challenging
shows, and attempts to blow away some of the myths surrounding lighting in this format.

Lighting the Stage *Francis Reid* **£14.95** ISBN 1904031080
Lighting the Stage discusses the human relationships involved in lighting design – both
between people, and between these people and technology. The book is written from a
highly personal viewpoint and its 'thinking aloud' approach is one that Francis Reid has
used in his writings over the past 30 years.

Model National Standard Conditions *ABTT/DSA/LGLA* **£20.00** ISBN 1904031110
These *Model National Standard Conditions* covers operational matters and complement *The
Technical Standards for Places of Entertainment*, which describes the physical requirements
for building and maintaining entertainment premises.

Mr Phipps' Theatre *Mark Jones, John Pick* **£17.95** ISBN: 1904031382
Mark Jones and John Pick describe "The Sensational Story of Eastbourne's Royal
Hippodrome" – formerly Eastbourne Theatre Royal. An intriguing narrative, the book sets
the story against a unique social history of the town. Peter Longman, former director of The
Theatres Trust, provides the Foreword.

Pages From Stages *Anthony Field* **£17.95** ISBN 1904031269
Anthony Field explores the changing style of theatres including interior design, exterior
design, ticket and seat prices, and levels of service, while questioning whether the theatre
still exists as a place of entertainment for regular theatre-goers.

Performing Arts Technical Training Handbook 2007/2008 *ed: John Offord* **£19.95** ISBN
9781904031451
Published in association with the ABTT (Association of British Theatre Technicians), this
important Handbook includes fully detailed and indexed entries describing courses on
backstage crafts offered by over 100 universities and colleges across the UK. A completely
new research project, with accompanying website, the title also includes articles with advice
for those considering a career 'behind the scenes', together with contact information and
descriptions of the major organisations involved with industry training – plus details of
companies offering training within their own premises. The Handbook will be kept in print,
with a major revision annually.

Practical Dimming *Nick Mobsby* **£22.95** ISBN 19040313447
This important and easy to read title covers the history of electrical and electronic dimming,
how dimmers work, current dimmer types from around the world, planning of a dimming
system, looking at new sine wave dimming technology and distributed dimming. Integration
of dimming into different performance venues as well as the necessary supporting electrical
systems are fully detailed. Significant levels of information are provided on the many
different forms and costs of potential solutions as well as how to plan specific solutions.
Architectural dimming for the likes of hotels, museums and shopping centres are included.
Practical Dimming is a companion book to Practical DMX and is designed for all involved
in the use, operation and design of dimming systems.

Practical DMX *Nick Mobsby* **£16.95** ISBN 1904031368
In this highly topical and important title the author details the principles of DMX, how to plan a network, how to choose equipment and cables, with data on products from around the world, and how to install DMX networks for shows and on a permanently installed basis. The easy style of the book and the helpful fault finding tips, together with a review of different DMX testing devices provide an ideal companion for all lighting technicians and system designers. An introduction to Ethernet and Canbus networks are provided as well tips on analogue networks and protocol conversion. This title has been recently updated to include a new chapter on Remote Device Management that became an international standard in Summer 2006.

Practical Guide to Health and Safety in the Entertainment Industry
Marco van Beek **£14.95** ISBN 1904031048
This book is designed to provide a practical approach to Health and Safety within the Live Entertainment and Event industry. It gives industry-pertinent examples, and seeks to break down the myths surrounding Health and Safety.

Production Management *Joe Aveline* **£17.95** ISBN 1904031102
Joe Aveline's book is an in-depth guide to the role of the Production Manager, and includes real-life practical examples and 'Aveline's Fables' – anecdotes of his experiences with real messages behind them.

Rigging for Entertainment: Regulations and Practice *Chris Higgs* **£19.95**
ISBN 1904031218
Continuing where he left off with his highly successful *An Introduction to Rigging in the Entertainment Industry*, Chris Higgs' second title covers the regulations and use of equipment in greater detail.

Rock Solid Ethernet *Wayne Howell* **£24.95** ISBN 1904031293
Although aimed specifically at specifiers, installers and users of entertainment industry systems, this book will give the reader a thorough grounding in all aspects of computer networks, whatever industry they may work in. The inclusion of historical and technical 'sidebars' make for an enjoyable as well as informative read.

Sixty Years of Light Work *Fred Bentham* **£26.95** ISBN 1904031072
This title is an autobiography of one of the great names behind the development of modern stage lighting equipment and techniques.

Sound for the Stage *Patrick Finelli* **£24.95** ISBN 1904031153
Patrick Finelli's thorough manual covering all aspects of live and recorded sound for performance is a complete training course for anyone interested in working in the field of stage sound, and is a must for any student of sound.

Stage Lighting Design in Britain: The Emergence of the Lighting Designer, 1881-1950 *Nigel Morgan* **£17.95** ISBN 190403134X
This book sets out to ascertain the main course of events and the controlling factors that determined the emergence of the theatre lighting designer in Britain, starting with the introduction of incandescent electric light to the stage, and ending at the time of the first public lighting design credits around 1950. The book explores the practitioners, equipment, installations and techniques of lighting design.

Stage Lighting for Theatre Designers *Nigel Morgan* **£17.95** ISBN 1904031196
This is an updated second edition of Nigel Morgan's popular book for students of theatre design – outlining all the techniques of stage lighting design.

Technical Marketing Techniques *David Brooks, Andy Collier, Steve Norman* **£24.95** ISBN 190403103X
Technical Marketing is a novel concept, recently defined and elaborated by the authors of this book, with business-to-business companies competing in fast developing technical product sectors.

Technical Standards for Places of Entertainment *ABTT/DSA* **£30.00** ISBN 1904031056
Technical Standards for Places of Entertainment details the necessary physical standards required for entertainment venues.

Theatre Engineering and Stage Machinery *Toshiro Ogawa* **£30.00** ISBN 9781904031024
Theatre Engineering and Stage Machinery is a unique reference work covering every aspect of theatrical machinery and stage technology in global terms, and across the complete historical spectrum. Revised February 2007.

Theatre Lighting in the Age of Gas *Terence Rees* **£24.95** ISBN 190403117X
Entertainment Technology Press has republished this valuable historic work previously produced by the Society for Theatre Research in 1978. *Theatre Lighting in the Age of Gas* investigates the technological and artistic achievements of theatre lighting engineers from the 1700s to the late Victorian period.

Theatre Space: A Rediscovery Reported *Francis Reid* **£19.95** ISBN 1904031439
In the post-war world of the 1950s and 60s, the format of theatre space became a matter for a debate that aroused passions of an intensity unknown before or since. The proscenium arch was clearly identified as the enemy, accused of forming a barrier to disrupt the relations between the actor and audience. An uneasy fellow-traveller at the time, Francis Reid later recorded his impressions whilst enjoying performances or working in theatres old and new and this book is an important collection of his writings in various theatrical journals from 1969-2001 including his contribution to the Cambridge Guide to the Theatre in 1988. It reports some of the flavour of the period when theatre architecture was rediscovering its past in a search to establish its future.

Theatres of Achievement *John Higgins* **£29.95** ISBN: 1904031374
John Higgins affectionately describes the history of 40 distinguished UK theatres in a personal tribute, each uniquely illustrated by the author. Completing each profile is colour photography by Adrian Eggleston.

Theatric Tourist *Francis Reid* **£19.95** ISBN 9781904031468
Theatric Tourist is the delightful story of Francis Reid's visits across more than 50 years to theatres, theatre museums, performances and even movie theme parks. In his inimitable style, the author involves the reader within a personal experience of venues from the Legacy of Rome to theatres of the Renaissance and Eighteenth Century Baroque and the Gustavian Theatres of Stockholm. His performance experiences include Wagner in Beyreuth, the Pleasures of Tivoli and Wayang in Singapore. This is a 'must have' title for those who are as "incurably stagestruck" as the author.

Walt Disney Concert Hall – The Backstage Story *Patricia MacKay & Richard Pilbrow*
£28.95 ISBN 1904031234
Spanning the 16-year history of the design and construction of the Walt Disney Concert Hall, this book provides a fresh and detailed behind the scenes story of the design and technology from a variety of viewpoints. This is the first book to reveal the "process" of the design of a concert hall.

Yesterday's Lights – A Revolution Reported *Francis Reid* **£26.95** ISBN 1904031323
Set to help new generations to be aware of where the art and science of theatre lighting is coming from – and stimulate a nostalgia trip for those who lived through the period, Francis Reid's latest book has over 350 pages dedicated to the task, covering the 'revolution' from the fifties through to the present day. Although this is a highly personal account of the development of lighting design and technology and he admits that there are 'gaps', you'd be hard put to find anything of significance missing.

Go to www.etbooks.co.uk for full details of above titles and secure online ordering facilities.